The Great Adventure
Exploring Christian Faith with Young People

Patricia Bays

Anglican Book Centre
Toronto, Canada

1997
Anglican Book Centre
600 Jarvis Street
Toronto, Ontario
M4Y 2J6

Cover illustration: Michael Engel
Cover design, text design and illustrations: Saskia Rowley

Grateful acknowlegement is made for permission to reprint excerpts from copyrighted material, including the following:

A Wind in the Door by Madeleine L'Engle. Copyright © 1973 by Crosswicks, Ltd. Reprinted by permission of Farrar, Straus & Giroux, Inc.
I Am David by Ann Holm. Reprinted by permission of Reed Books.
"Bakerwoman God" from *Womanpriest: A Personal Odyssey* by Allah Bozarth-Campbell. Copyright © 1978 by Allah Bozarth-Campbell. Reprinted by permission of Paulist Press.
The Best Christmas Pageant Ever by Barbara Robinson. Copyright © 1972 by Barbara Robinson. Reprinted by permission of HarperCollins Publishers.
The Velveteen Rabbit by Margery Williams. Reprinted by permission of Reed Books.
The Lemming Condition by Alan Arkin. Text copyright © 1976 by Alan Arkin. Reprinted by permission of HarperCollins Publishers.
A Wrinkle in Time by Madeleine L'Engle. Copyright © 1962 by Crosswicks, Ltd. Copyright renewed © by Madeleine L'Engle Franklin. Reprinted by permission of Farrar, Straus & Giroux, Inc.
The Silver Chair by C. S. Lewis. Reprinted by permission of HarperCollins Publishers.

Canadian Cataloguing in Publication Data

Bays, Patricia
    The great adventure

ISBN 1-55126-176-6

1. Christian education of children.
2. Christian education of teenagers.
3. Activity programs in Christian education.
I. Title.

BV1475.2.B39 1997   268'.432   C97-930029-0

The Great Adventure

Table of Contents

Acknowledgements   6

Introduction   7

Introduction for the Leader   11
    Worksheet 1: Planning Guide   20
    Worksheet 2: Planning the Theme   21

Beginning the Program   23
    Worksheet 3: Getting to Know You   25
    Worksheet 4: Scavenger Hunt Bingo   26

Theme One: Belonging   27
    Worksheet 5: On Baptism   36

Theme Two: God   45

Theme Three: Jesus   63

Theme Four: The Church   77
    Worksheet 6: Research Projects   81
    Worksheet 7: The Eucharist   87

Theme Five: The Christian Life   93

Appendix: What Does It Mean To Be an Anglican?   109

Resources   125

Acknowledgements

Special thanks to Sue Kargut, Marilyn Dean, and Marlene Haygarth for reading the manuscript and suggesting ideas and resources;

to Raye Hendrickson for helping me test the material with a class of young people at St Paul's Cathedral, Regina, and for suggesting new approaches and ideas for using the content;

to the young people of St Paul's Cathedral, Lauren Bamford, Cassie Bolingbroke, Crystal Lysyk, Andrew and Jennifer Melville, Bridget and Kristie Patterson, Angela Stolz and Nathaniel Weller, whose enthusiasm and liveliness made it all worthwhile;

to Susan Graham Walker, Janet Marshall Eibner, and Patti Carlisle for reading and commenting on the manuscript;

to the editorial and production staff of the Anglican Book Centre, particularly James Mainprize, Elizabeth Phinney, Saskia Rowley, and Robert Maclennan, for all the care and attention they gave to this book; and

to Eric, Jonathan, and Becky for their love and encouragement.

Introduction

At the present time, Anglicans around the world are discussing the meaning and importance of rites of initiation. What does baptism mean? What does it mean to say that baptism confers full membership in the body of Christ? Should young children be admitted to the Eucharist? How does such admission affect the rite of confirmation? What is the place of confirmation in today's church? These questions are providing the fuel for much lively discussion at many levels of church life.

At the same time that this discussion is taking place, however, current Anglican practice in the parish still sees large numbers of adolescents seeking confirmation. To some extent, this may be due to parental expectation, yet in many cases it is the young people themselves who wish to take this step.

I have long been aware of the lack of print resources available for the education of adolescent confirmation candidates. That which is available is British or American in tone and does not entirely fit our Canadian culture.

At one time, confirmation instruction was defined as the handing on of a particular body of information. Students were instructed in the Catechism, often in its traditional question-and-answer memory work mode, and were allowed to come before the bishop once they had mastered the material. Some printed material still exists which follows this format, usually found in a short-answer workbook. This type of material reflects a content-centred style of education in which the teacher, who knows all the answers, gives them to the student, who doesn't. In some ways, this approach to teaching is easy for the teacher—the task is defined and the results are measurable.

In education today, we have moved to other models. We place less emphasis on the transmission of content than we do on the joint exploration by teacher and students of the gospel, and what it means in our lives. Both students and leaders are members of the Body of Christ, exploring together the content of the Christian revelation and learning from each other. The teacher contributes life experience and some preparation in terms of content, but the student also brings his or her accumulated knowledge and experience to share. The results are harder to measure, but are nonetheless real.

This material is written to help young Canadian Anglicans explore the Christian faith. Within this book, you will find both theological background and a wide range of activities to help students aged ten to fifteen to examine Christian beliefs at this stage in their faith development. It is not a detailed course of study, but rather a collection of resources from which the leader can build a program which meets the needs of a particular group of students. You will need to buy this book for the leader; the Worksheets within may be photocopied for the students. You will need to purchase craft materials, and provide children's literature and music. The parish may wish to buy these resources to start a professional collection for teachers, or the leader might find them in public or school libraries. The section on page 125 lists the resources that are needed.

The Great Adventure is designed to be used with *The Book of Alternative Services*. The rites of Christian initiation (baptism, confirmation, the renewal of baptismal vows at the Easter vigil) within *The Book of Alternative Services* are among its strongest and are widely used by Anglican parishes. Parishes using services from *The Book of Common Prayer* will need to adapt this material in order to use it for confirmation preparation.

Principles

The material in *The Great Adventure* is based on certain theological and educational principles:

- Baptism conveys full membership in the church. Therefore children and young people are current (not future) members of the church and share with adults in its life, worship, and work.

- Confirmation is an important sacramental rite by which young people reaffirm for themselves the baptismal promises made on their behalf in infancy, and make a commitment to appropriate adult ministry in the church and in everyday life.

- Adults, adolescents, and children are all growing in the faith. Everyone is a learner. Christian Education is lifelong.

- There are many different learning styles. Some people learn by thought and reflection. Some people learn best by doing, by hands-on activity. Some of us learn best through our eyes, by what we read and see. Some of us learn better through our ears, by what we hear.

- There are different teaching styles. Some teachers need the security of a structured program, with clear content. Others are more comfortable responding to the questions and needs of the students.

Learning through Literature

An important feature of this material is its use of literature to explore the Christian faith. The reading of fiction and poetry has always been an important way in which to learn about God, about the human soul, about the struggles of good and evil. This reading should never be dismissed as frivolous, as it allows us to use our imaginations in the search for God, to expand our vision, and to view life from a different perspective. In *Of Other Worlds*, C. S. Lewis speaks of imagination as "the organ of meaning." "Literature," he says, "at its best can do more, it can give us experiences we have never had and thus, instead of commenting on life, can add to it" (p. 38).

In C. S. Lewis's *George Macdonald: An Anthology*, fantasy writer George MacDonald says of good literature that "it arouses in us sensations we have never had before, never anticipated having—it gets under our skin, hits us at a level deeper than our thoughts or even our passions, troubles oldest certainties till all questions are re-opened, and in general shocks us more fully awake than we are for most of our lives" (pp. 16–17). What a wonderful thing—to be shocked more fully awake, more aware of the world around us, of the experience of other people, of how God meets us every day.

Katherine Paterson, a missionary child and a clergy wife, writes excellent fiction for young people and has also written volumes of criticism. In *Gates of Excellence*, she says that she writes fiction because "fiction allows us to do something nothing else quite does. It allows us to enter fully into the lives of other human beings" (p. 58). Of novels, she states that "a great novel is a kind of conversion experience. We come away from it changed" (p. 59). She sees a novelist as a "spy for hope" and perhaps, as teachers and parents, that is our calling too.

This curriculum resource draws on children's books to help to explore faith issues and to involve the imagination in our search for God. Some of the best books being written today are books for children and young people. There are some fine authors exploring the meaning of good and evil, what it is like to live with ambiguity, and the difficulty of making decisions in our complex world.

The Leader

The leader may be clergy or lay, but should be someone with an interest in exploring faith with adolescents. The leader should be flexible, and able to put together a program by picking and choosing from among the suggested resources to meet the needs and interests of a particular group of students. Some theological knowledge and understanding is necessary, as the background material included here cannot provide an in-depth study of all the doctrines and issues of the Christian faith. The section on resources at the back of the book lists additional helpful material.

Introduction for the Leader

The Great Adventure seeks to provide a sufficient variety of materials to meet the needs of both you and your students. There is no single plan for exploring a theme; as leader, you will need to choose activities and resources which meet the needs and interests of the students. The program will thus be different each time you teach it.

The material can be used for confirmation classes, but may also be adapted for summer camp, youth groups, church school, or weekend events.

The Learner

People learn in many different ways. There is no single style of learning which is correct or better than others. Here are some of the differences.

Some people are energized by being with others. They like to engage in conversation and share ideas, and to participate in group activities. They develop and refine their own ideas by testing them against the ideas of others. They often think out loud and have a ready answer to any question.

Some people are drained by being with others. They have learned to get along in groups but need some time alone to recover their energy. They develop and refine their ideas by thinking them over quietly, on their own. They need an opportunity to reflect before they offer an opinion.

Some people learn by hands-on experience: building something, playing a game, acting in a play. Too much discussion and reflection leaves them cold. They like factual details, concrete examples, a sequential story.

Some people like the challenge of playing around with ideas, fitting concepts into an overall pattern. Discussion and journal writing are their cups of tea. They like fantasy, metaphor, the exploration of what is possible.

Some people learn through hearing: listening to a story, seeing a play performed, reading aloud.

Some people learn by reading for themselves: using charts and diagrams, writing a diary.

Some people are eager to approach what is new and try out new activities and situations without hesitation.

Some people are more hesitant to try the new and unfamiliar.

The atmosphere in which we learn also plays a vital role. Is this group welcoming? Can I trust this group to accept what I reveal of myself? Does the teacher have a "hidden agenda," a destination where we are supposed to end up? Or is it okay for me to share my questions and doubts?

Take the time to get to know your students and their different styles.

Characteristics of Age Groups

There is a vast difference between youth of ten years of age and those of fifteen years of age. The younger children are still in elementary school. Fifteen-year-olds are in their senior years at high school and well on their way to adulthood.

Junior students, ages ten and eleven, have plenty of energy. They like to ask questions, do projects, work in groups. They have reading and writing skills and good background knowledge, and are not yet afraid to reveal their curiosity and enthusiasm. They have a strong need to belong to the group so many of the themes of this course will fit them well.

Older students, ages twelve to fifteen, are going through many physical and psychological changes. They may feel awkward and self-conscious. This is a time of questioning adult values and coming to an understanding of who they are as unique individuals. Young people need acceptance and support, and a safe place to raise questions and concerns.

If they are considering being confirmed, students of both age groups need to be assured that proceeding to confirmation is their own decision and not that of parents or grandparents. The leader may need to speak with the parents to support a young person's decision not to be confirmed at this stage.

The Teacher

Like the students, leaders also have different styles of learning, and different styles of teaching. Consider the following questions:

1. Reflect on a recent experience of learning something new—a class you took, a new skill you learned. What kind of things helped you to learn?

2. What makes a good learning environment for you? Quiet time or groups of people? Hands-on experience or playing around with ideas? Books and writing? Audio material? What kind of structure do you need to learn?

3. Think of people whom you would describe as good teachers. What makes them effective? Why did you learn from them? How then would you describe your own learning style? What sort of teaching style do you find most comfortable?

Remember to look at team teaching as an option. Each teacher can then build on individual strengths. Joint planning and shared leadership during the class can enrich the learning experience for all.

William Temple said, "The subject matter is the student." What are your hopes for these students? What kind of experiences would you like them to have?

Remember to pray each week for your students. Take a little time to think of each one, their homes and families, the community in which you live. Ask God to bless them and to guide your learning together.

Project Model

The model of education used in this program is the project model—a variety of ideas and activities to explore a particular theme. Think of the theme as being situated at the centre of a web. Around the centre, and connected to it, are the many ways to explore the theme.

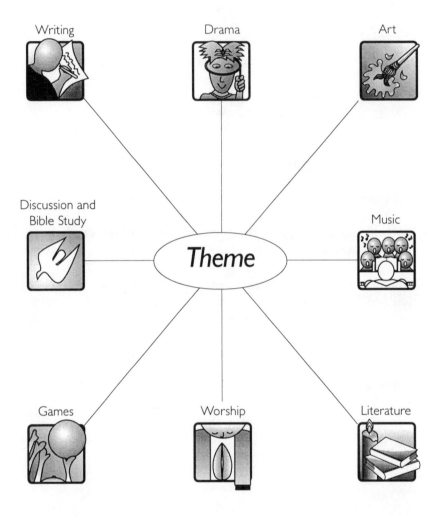

Writing

Drama

Art

Discussion and
Bible Study

Theme

Music

Games

Worship

Literature

Some groups of young people will enjoy drama and music and find these effective ways of experiencing a rich appreciation of the theme. Members of other groups may feel very uncomfortable having to perform, but will enjoy discussion or art or writing in reflecting on the theme. Choose activities with which both you and your group feel comfortable, and ask the students to help you select them. Choose as many or as few activities as will help you explore the theme together. Further information about planning is found on pages 18–21 .

How to Use a Novel or Story in Teaching

Some of the suggested activities in this program involve using novels with children. Ideally, it is best if everyone can read the novel in preparation for the activity. There are some short novels, such as *The Velveteen Rabbit*, which can be read aloud in about twenty minutes and then used as a basis for discussion or other activities.

Other novels are longer and need to be read at home. If you have a group of keen readers, they might take one of the suggested books and read it as a basis for discussion and activities. I have included excerpts from these novels in this resource, along with an introduction to the story. I suggest that you tell the students a bit about the background of the story, and read aloud to them the excerpt printed in this material. Then use the discussion questions with the students. Those who get excited by the excerpt may decide to find the book in their school or public library, and continue reading for themselves.

How to Read a Picture Book

There are many fine picture books for children in which very profound concepts are explored in a brief space. Reading a picture book, even to a group of adults, provides everyone in the group with a common experience. For a few moments, the whole class shares in the reading and can then discuss the ideas which the book brings to light. Older children may wonder if reading a picture book together is a bit babyish; you may need to introduce this part of the lesson carefully. School librarians have been using picture books with older children for some years, so you will probably find that your students are quite comfortable with the medium. I have read picture books aloud in sermons, at adult education events, at retreats, and with groups of teenagers. In every case, listeners were quickly drawn into the story and absorbed by its message.

Sit where everyone can see the pictures in the book. If the amount of text is slight, you may want to hold the book sideways so that everyone can see as you read. Or you may want to read a page and then hold the pictures up for all to look at.

Vary the presentation. Students may take turns reading the book aloud, or a group of students may dramatize the story. The book can be left out for students to examine and re-read.

Journal Writing

It is suggested that each student have a journal in which to record reflections on the theme, questions raised by the discussion, or ideas to pursue. You may wish to provide notebooks or have the students bring their own. You will need to agree as a class whether the journal is private or whether it may be shared with the class. If the journals are private, then there may be occasions when the students do some writing on sheets of paper with the intention of sharing these with the group. The students might write letters to the leader, sharing thoughts and concerns on a particular topic.

Brainstorming

Brainstorming is a technique used to generate a large number of ideas. There are certain rules to follow:
- Set a time limit. Two or three minutes should give you a good list.
- Record all ideas on newsprint or a blackboard.
- The object is quantity, so encourage students to suggest as many ideas as they can.
- Allow no evaluation, as it interrupts the flow of ideas. Simply write all answers on the board.
- Encourage creativity and far-out ideas.
- Piggy-back on the ideas of others. Take them a step further.

Worship

Worship is an important part of class time. Plan this with your students. Ask them to share in the responsibility for opening and closing prayers. Some of the themes explore the worship of the church, so you may want to use some of those prayers to reinforce the learnings that are taking place. Music and movement are important aspects of worship too. The theme materials will give you some ideas, but feel free to add your own and those of the students. Brainstorm with the students for ideas for intercessions and litanies. Involve the students in preparing and leading worship.

The Themes

Theme One: Belonging
We belong to the human family by God's gift of creation. We belong to the Christian family through our baptism. What does it mean to belong?

Theme Two: God
We believe in God who created us and the universe, and who sustains us in being. Together we explore who God is and what that means for us.

Theme Three: Jesus
We believe in God who redeemed us through the life, death, and resurrection of Jesus the beloved Son. Who is Jesus and what does his life mean for us today?

In themes 2 and 3, we think also about God the Holy Spirit. We believe that God as Spirit strengthens and empowers us for life in the world and in the church.

Theme Four: The Church
We are called to be part of the family of the church. What does membership in the church require from us?

Theme Five: The Christian Life
We are called to live as Christians in our everyday life. How can we follow Jesus in the life of the schoolroom and the sports team and at home?

Each theme is accompanied by the following material:

1. *The theological background of the theme.* This is information to help you, the leader, understand what is being taught in this section of the program. This is not lecture material to be read to the students. Rather, it is a way to help you start sorting out your own ideas on the theme. The material may raise questions for you, and you may want to explore these first through other reading (see the bibliography for some ideas) and by talking with others who are engaged in teaching.

2. *The web.* A diagram sets out a variety of options for exploring the theme. Choose one or more of these activities (with the help of your students) which are of interest to you and your group.

3. A description of the various activities, with a list of necessary supplies.

4. Other resources and suggestions.

5. Some prayers and ideas for worship.

Each theme could occupy several sessions, so you will need to sit down and do some planning. (Use Worksheet 1, "Planning Guide" and Worksheet 2, "Planning the Theme" on pages 20 and 21.) The program may differ with each group you lead.

How to Plan

In planning, there are a number of factors to consider:
• the number of students
• their ages and interests
• the number of weeks available (6 weeks? 12 weeks?)

- the pattern of meeting (once a week, four Saturdays, a couple of weekends, a week at summer camp?)
- the length of each session (1 hour, 2 hours?)
- the meeting space (Is there room for games, drama, music? Will you have a video player, a cassette player? What are the possibilities for field trips?)
- the number of helpers available.

Raye Hendrickson, a member and fellow educator at St Paul's Cathedral in Regina, and I tested the material with a class of nine young persons. The sessions we planned were three hours in length. We quickly learned that this was far too long both for leaders and students! We settled on two-hour sessions, with a break for a snack. We found that we needed to plan a good variety of activities during that time, to keep the pace moving along. Sessions of one hour to one and one-half hours will probably be best with your group.

A group meeting once a week for ten weeks might plan to spend two sessions on each theme.

Here is a sample plan for exploring the first theme, "Belonging."

Week One

1. Opening Activity—group building game	15 min
2. Literature/discussion—*The Hockey Sweater*	20
3. Snack	10
4. Drama—role plays	30
5. Music	10
6. Closing Worship	5
	90

Week Two

1. Music	10
2. Discussion: Baptismal Covenant	20
3. Snack	10
4. Art—Collage	30
5. Co-operative game	15
6. Closing Reflection: *On the Day You Were Born*	5
	90

Worksheet 1: *Planning Guide*

Date: _____

Theme One: Belonging
Week 1 _____
Week 2 _____
Week 3 _____

Theme Two: God
Week 1 _____
Week 2 _____
Week 3 _____

Theme Three: Jesus
Week 1 _____
Week 2 _____
Week 3 _____

Theme Four: The Christian Life
Week 1 _____
Week 2 _____
Week 3 _____

Theme Five: The Church
Week 1 _____
Week 2 _____
Week 3 _____

Date of Confirmation or Windup: _____

Worksheet 2: *Planning the Theme*

Theme Title: _____

Session	Activities	Materials Required

Supplies You Will Need

Art
Mural paper
Drawing paper
Construction paper
Markers, pencil crayons, crayons
Clay (look for self-firing clay at a teachers' supply store)
Glue or glue sticks

Books
Bibles
The Book of Alternative Services
Picture books and novels

Journals
Notebooks and pens

Discussion supplies
Newsprint
Markers
Masking tape
Photocopies of worksheets

Music
Hymn books or song books
Cassette player and tapes as indicated in lesson
> Would you feel comfortable saying grace in the lunchroom? In a restaurant?
> What are some of the ways in which young Christian people can make a difference?
> Is there a down side to this? What are some of the problems that being a Christian might cause you?

4. Have the students develop role plays about situations in which it is difficult to be a Christian.

Beginning the Program

Your students may not be well acquainted with one another. They may go to different schools, be in different grades, even live in different communities. Their only connection may be that their families are members of this particular parish. Furthermore, they may not know you well. So at the beginning of the program you may need to take time to help the students get to know one another and you. They will need activities which help them to feel a part of a group or a team, so give some thought as to how you might accomplish this. Here are some ideas:

1. At the first session, spend some time on a "Getting to Know You" activity. Worksheet 3 on page 25, "Getting to Know You," is a sample information sheet for each student to fill out. This will provide you with their addresses and phone numbers, and acquaint you with their interests.

2. Worksheet 4, "Scavenger Hunt Bingo," found on page 26, will help the students learn more about one another.

3. Ask the students to find one other person whom they do not know well and interview them about their likes and dislikes. Allow time for the second person to interview their partner. Then, within the circle of the whole group, ask each student to introduce their partner. If there is an odd number of students, have that student interview you and vice versa.

4. Have students share their expectations for the program. Ask them to tell the group why they have come to the program, and what they hope it will be like. Use this information to help you plan for subsequent sessions.

5. Plan activities that will help to build the team. You may want to choose a name for the group. The "Handprint" collage (see page 38) can be displayed in a prominent place so that the students and the parish develop a sense of the group's identity.

Worksheet 3: *Getting to Know You*

Name _____

Address _____

Phone _____

Age _____ Birthday _____Grade _____

Brothers and Sisters _____

Pets _____

My favourite food _____

My favourite music _____

What I like best about school _____

What I would like to change about school _____

If I could do anything I want on a Saturday, I would _____
_____

Hobbies I enjoy _____

My favourite book _____

My favourite movie _____

My favourite television show _____

Worksheet 4: *Scavenger Hunt Bingo*

someone born in another province or country	someone wearing blue socks	someone who plays a musical instrument
someone who has a pet	**BINGO**	someone who is born in the same month as you
someone who plays basketball	someone who is the eldest child	someone who is wearing a belt

Theme One
Belonging

Introduction

We begin with the theme of belonging for both practical and theological reasons. In bringing a class of learners together for a period of time, we are forming a group of those who are strangers to one another. Helping this diverse group learn and grow together is a practical exploration of what belonging means. In this first theme we want to include activities which encourage getting to know one another. Group-building activities and co-operative games are important parts of the early sessions. We want to help students experience belonging as they reflect on what it means to belong to the Christian family.

Belonging is also an important place to begin in theological terms. By baptism we are "made one with Christ in His death and resurrection," and "brought to new birth in the family of the Church." Baptism is about belonging to God and belonging to one another. So baptism takes place at public worship, when the community is gathered. The candidate or sponsors make promises to live the new life in Christ, and the gathered community also makes promises to sustain this person in this new life. Confirmation, taking responsibility for these promises and receiving gifts of the Spirit for ministry in the world, is directly related to the baptismal covenant. Therefore, this theme includes an exploration of baptism and what it means to belong to the church.

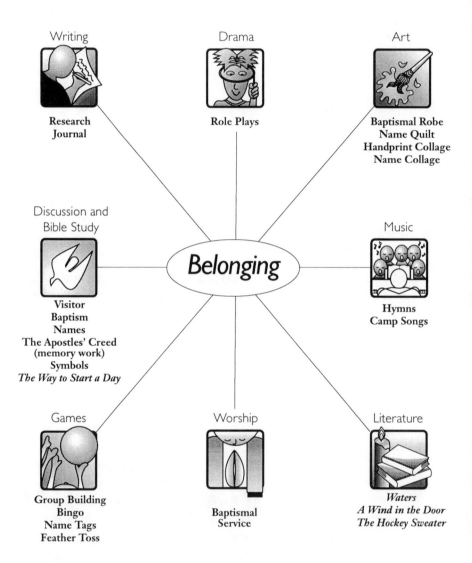

Writing
Research
Journal

Drama
Role Plays

Art
Baptismal Robe
Name Quilt
Handprint Collage
Name Collage

Discussion and
Bible Study
Visitor
Baptism
Names
The Apostles' Creed
(memory work)
Symbols
The Way to Start a Day

Belonging

Music
Hymns
Camp Songs

Games
Group Building
Bingo
Name Tags
Feather Toss

Worship
Baptismal
Service

Literature
Waters
A Wind in the Door
The Hockey Sweater

Group-Building Activities

1. Have each student print his or her name on a piece of construction paper and decorate the tag with several symbols that are important to them. Suggestions might include a favourite food, hobby, sport, music, or colour. After ten minutes, ask students to locate another person in the group whose name tag shows that they have something in common. Have them sit down together, find out more about each other, and then introduce each other to the group. At this stage, you may want to include a discussion of names, and their meaning and importance. See page 41.

2. Use one of the "Getting to Know You" activities on page 23. For example, make enough copies of the Bingo sheet and give students five minutes to fill in names. Or have each student interview and introduce another class member.

Literature

The Hockey Sweater by Roch Carrier. Read this book aloud to the students. Here is a summary of the story:

> In the winter of 1946, all the village boys play hockey. All wear Montreal Canadiens' sweaters and dream of being like Maurice Richard. When the narrator outgrows his sweater, his mother orders a new one from Eaton's. To everyone's horror, Monsieur Eaton sends a blue and white Toronto Maple Leafs' sweater! His mother insists that he wear the hated sweater, but his team mates refuse to let him play. When his temper explodes, the curate sends him off to church to pray for forgiveness. He asks God to

send a hundred million moths to eat up the Maple Leafs'
sweater.

1. Discuss the following questions with the students:
   Why was the narrator so upset about the Maple Leafs
   sweater?
   Why do you think his mother acted as she did?
   What other things could the boy have done?
   Has anything like this ever happened to you?

2. Ask the students to find a partner. In pairs, ask them to talk about
   a time when they felt that they didn't belong. How did that feel?
   What did they do?

3. Place several newsprint sheets on the wall. Ask students to com-
   plete these sentences:
   I know that I belong in my family when...
   I know that I belong at school when...

Journal

1. Introduce the idea of the journal to the students and explain that
   this will be an ongoing activity. Establish the ground rules: Will
   they work on the journal in class or at home? Will the writing be
   private or shared?

2. Give the students some class time to write down their thoughts
   about belonging. Ask them:
   When have you felt that you didn't belong?
   How did you handle it?
   When do you feel that you really belong?

Drama and Role Plays

The following improvisations are designed to help students experience exclusion or inclusion. Remember to conclude the activity by having the students return to you the roles that they have taken on. You need to indicate that the role play is over, so that the student who is playing the role of one who is excluded does not continue to feel outside the group.

1. Have two or three students mime an activity—a game of catch, a conversation, a household task. Ask another student to stand outside the group. Have the group mime including the newcomer and giving him or her something to do.

2. Choose and have the group act out a family activity in which all family members have something to do and feel included. Suggested activities may include preparing dinner, or packing the car for a trip.

3. Have the students role-play a situation in which someone is excluded from a group. Then do the role play again, this time including that student in the group. Ask:
   How did you as a group member or as the outsider feel in each of those situations?

Co-operative Games

Many of the games we play are competitive. They encourage us to compete against others and to win by defeating the other players or the other team. Co-operative games encourage players to work together. They encourage everyone, no matter what their ability, to take part and to contribute to the game, and thus encourage a sense of belonging.

Feather Toss
Ask the students to form a circle and join hands. Throw feathers into the air and have the players blow in order to keep them there. If the group is too large, divide the students into two circles. You might want to time the group's effort using a stopwatch.

A good source of co-operative games is the Canadian company "Family Pastimes," which makes and sells board games and puzzles for all ages. Write for their catalogue at R. R. # 4, Perth, ON K7H 3C6.

Baptism

Introduction

As part of your preparation, read the introduction on pages 146–149 of *The Book of Alternative Services (BAS)*. This will provide useful theological and biblical background material.

Baptism is an act of the church by which an individual is given the gift of new life and becomes part of the Christian community. It is a sacrament, an "outward and visible sign of an inward and spiritual grace." By the outward and visible sign of water, we are given the inward and spiritual grace of new life in Christ by God's Spirit, and are made members of Christ's body, the church.

Page 150 contains rubrics or directions for the service. The word *rubric* means "red," a traditional colour for printing directions in prayer books. Pages 163 to 165 contain additional directions.

The Liturgy

A Walk through the BAS *Baptismal Service.*

Give a copy of the *BAS* to each student and walk through the service with them, using the information given under each heading below. Outline the headings on newsprint. Or divide the students into four groups and have them research the questions on the Worksheet (page 36), using the *BAS*. Have them record their answers on newsprint to share their research with the class. The questions are designed to help them become familiar with *The Book of Alternative Services* so that they understand the pattern and elements of worship. Questions for discussion of the meaning of baptism follow the Worksheet.

1. *The Gathering of the Community* (p. 151).
Baptism incorporates us into the body of Christ. The dialogue between celebrant (the priest) and people calls the community together, and the Collect of the Day gathers up ("collects") our prayers and focuses our thoughts.

2. *The Proclamation of the Word* (p. 152).
We listen to the readings from the Scriptures, and we hear the Word broken open by the preacher and shared with us. Normally the readings of the day are used at baptism. You will find the lectionary (the list of readings for Sundays) along with the Collect and other prayers on pages 268–431 of the *BAS*. The Canadian Church Calendar gives the name and season for each Sunday. The Revised Common Lectionary, adopted in 1995, is printed separately in such books as the *Order of Divine Service* or the *Canadian Church Desk Diary*.

3. *The Presentation and Examination of Candidates* (pp. 153–156).
Baptism requires promises from those who are old enough to speak for themselves. These promises are found on page 154. We promise to renounce evil and turn to Jesus Christ.

Because baptism means incorporation into the Christian family, the church baptizes infants when other Christians are willing to make these promises on their behalf. Parents or godparents or sponsors make the promises for the infant.

At one time, baptisms took place at private services with only the immediate family and friends present. We have now come to understand that baptism is never a private matter. Baptism makes us members of the community of faith and so should take place in the context of the worshipping congregation. The congregation prays that the candidates may be given strength to keep the promises and to lead a Christian life, and later welcomes the newly baptized into their community.

4. *Thanksgiving over the Water* (pp. 156–158).
References to water recur in many places in the Bible. With your students, trace the many references in these prayers: the creation (Genesis 1:1–8), the exodus (Exodus 14:10–31), Jesus' baptism (Mark 1:9–11). The picture book *God Speaks to Us in Water Stories* offers a good selection of stories. Water symbolizes cleansing. It is essential for sustaining life. We float in the water of the womb before we are born; in baptism we are born to new life. Note the references to the Holy Spirit. Through God's gift of the Spirit, we are brought to new birth and strengthened to live the Christian life.

5. *The Baptismal Covenant* (pp. 158–159).
The whole congregation joins the candidates in reciting the Apostles' Creed, the early baptismal creed of the church. Each time a baptism is celebrated, we renew the promises made in our own baptism.

Examine each of the promises. What do they mean for our everyday lives? Is baptism only about church? How is the baptismal covenant lived out in the life of your parish in terms of worship, evangelism, pastoral care, social action?

6. *The Baptism* (pp. 160–161).
Baptism must have these essentials:
- the giving of the name
- water—the symbol of cleansing and rebirth (Water may be sprinkled or poured on the head, or the candidate may be immersed in the water.)

- in the name of the Trinity
- signing with the sign of the cross, sometimes with oil
- prayer for the gifts of the Spirit.

Light
A lighted candle may be given to the candidate. In the early church, baptisms took place at the Easter Vigil. The candidates entered the church in darkness and were baptized as the sun rose. The candle symbolizes our passage from death to life, from darkness to light. Discuss the symbol of light with the students.

Read aloud the picture book *The Way to Start a Day* by Byrd Baylor. Baylor says that the way to start the day is to greet the sun with a blessing or song. This book shows how people of many different times, places, and cultures honour the new day as the sun rises. "You have to make the sun happy.... You have to make a good world for it to live its one-day life in."

In the early church, candidates were given a new white robe as a sign of the new life. So those who are baptized today may wear special clothes to mark the occasion.

Worksheet 5: *On Baptism*

The Gathering of the Community/The Proclamation of the Word
(pp. 151–152)
1. Who is the celebrant?
2. How does the gathering differ from the customary greeting every Sunday? (page 185)
3. What is a Collect? Find the Collect for last Sunday.
4. From which parts of the Bible do we read? What are the lessons for next Sunday?
5. Why do you think the sermon comes where it does?

Presentation and Examination of Candidates (pp. 153–156)
1. Who presents the candidates?
2. What difference is there in presenting younger and older candidates?
3. What do the parents and godparents promise?
4. What do the candidates promise?
5. What things do we pray for?

Thanksgiving Over the Water (pp. 156–158)
The Baptismal Covenant (pp. 158–159)
1. What Bible stories about water are mentioned in the prayer?
2. According to the prayer on page 157, what happens in baptism?
3. What is the Baptismal Covenant? By what other name do we call it?
4. What are the five promises we all make every time there is a baptism?

The Baptism (pp. 160–161)
1. What happens during the baptism? (four things)
2. What two ways of using water are mentioned in the rubric?
3. What does "N" mean in the prayers?
4. What does the prayer for the newly baptized ask God to give?
5. Why does the congregation welcome the newly baptized?
6. The baptism service finishes with...

Discussion

1. You might want to discuss the following questions with the class:
   Should we baptize infants?
   How realistic are the promises that we are asked to make in baptism?
   If you are already baptized, has your baptism made a difference to you? What difference should it make?
   Do you feel that you belong in church? Why? Why not?

Research Project

1. Have the students find their baptismal certificate and bring it to class. Ask:
   When were you baptized?
   This is an important anniversary to celebrate. Using a large sheet of newsprint with twelve squares, make a calendar showing the baptismal dates of each student. Be sure to add your own date to the calendar.

2. Ask the students:
   Who are your godparents?
   Tell the students that their godparents would like to hear that he or she is taking this class. If the student is going to be confirmed, the godparents will want to come and help him or her celebrate this new stage in their Christian life.

3. Have the students ask their parents to tell them the story of their baptism and record it in their journal.

Some students may not be baptized but may be preparing for baptism at the time of the bishop's visit. Be sure to include them in the conversation too.

Art

Choose one art activity for each session of Theme One.

Baptismal Robe
1. Introduce this activity by telling the following to your students:
   In ancient times, when a person became a Druid (a religious leader of the early Celtic people), that person was given a plain white robe on which the symbols of his or her life as it unfolded would be embroidered. Early Christians wore a special, white, baptismal robe.

2. Ask the students:
   What symbols might have been embroidered on your baptismal robe?
   What symbols might be added in the future?

3. Have each student draw the outline of a robe on a large sheet of paper and add to it the symbols of important events and experiences in their life to this point. Or have each student bring an oversized white T-shirt to class. Using fabric paint or markers, ask them to decorate the shirt with appropriate symbols.

Handprint Collage
Each of us is a unique person; no two of us are alike.

1. Ask each student to trace an outline of their hand and then decorate it with appropriate symbols representing their likes, what is important to them, and how they would describe themselves. Fasten the hands to one large sheet of paper and entitle the collage,

"We Are All Unique." This could decorate the meeting space for the duration of the group.

Also see the "Name Collage" and "Name Quilt" activities on pages 41–42.

Video/Films

The video of *The Hockey Sweater* might be shown instead of reading the book. Your public library or school library may have a copy.

Music

If your group likes to sing, be sure to include music as part of your sessions. Many songs can be sung without accompaniment. Your students may be involved in choirs or play musical instruments, and this will give them a great opportunity to share their gifts with the class. You could also invite someone else from the community to help you with this part of the program.

1. Sing rounds as a way of showing that the voices of the whole group are richer than the individual voices. "Dona Nobis Pacem," "Gloria," "Seek Ye First" are some examples. You will find these songs in *Songs for a Gospel People*.

2. There are some camp songs in which voices are added in turn to create the harmony— "One Bottle of Pop," "The Instruments." *Spirit of Singing*, published by Wood Lake Books, is a good source of camp songs.

3. Sing some of the baptismal hymns. "Crashing Waters at Creation" is one of a number of new hymns for baptism found in *Common Praise of the Anglican Church of Canada, 1998*.

Prayer

1. Ask the students to look at the baptismal prayer in the *BAS* on page 160.
   We ask the Spirit to give us:
   • an inquiring and discerning heart
   • the courage to will and persevere
   • a spirit to know and love God
   • the gift of joy and wonder in all God's works.

   Talk about what each of these gifts means. Use the prayer as part of your closing worship for this session. Have the students memorize the prayer. Using magazine pictures, make a group collage of images to illustrate the prayer.

2. Introduce the *Anglican Cycle of Prayer*. The cycle lists daily prayers for one or two dioceses of the worldwide Anglican Communion, and is published each year by Forward Movement Publications. There should be a copy in every parish. If not, the book is easily available through church book stores. We are part of a wider community of Anglicans all over the world, and this book is a way of teaching us about the needs and concerns of our fellow Anglicans. Look up the date for the coming Sunday and share with the students the concerns for which we are asked to pray.

3. At one time students did a good deal of memorizing, both in Sunday school and in the secular school system. Committing parts of the liturgy and verses from Scripture to memory is a way of enriching the devotional life of the students. Those who attend church regularly will already know many of the responses by heart. If it seems appropriate, the Apostles' Creed could be recited together by the class and learned by heart. The prayer for the gifts of the Spirit (*BAS*, p. 160) is another piece of the baptismal liturgy which students might learn.

Names

The giving of the name is an important part of the baptism. It signifies that each of us is a unique individual, known to God by name. Bring a book which gives the meanings of names to class and allow the students to look up their own.

1. Ask the students:
   How do you feel about your name?
   What do you like to be called? Do you have a nickname that you like, that describes your personality?
   Were you named for anyone? For a saint or biblical character? For a relative?

2. A number of biblical people were given new names as a sign of a new beginning or change of direction in their lives. Look at some of these stories with your students.
   - Genesis 17:5—Abram (exalted ancestor) becomes Abraham (ancestor of a multitude)
   - Genesis 17:15—Sarai (God is prince) becomes Sarah (princess)
   - Genesis 35:10—Jacob (supplanter) becomes Israel (ruling with God)
   - Matthew 16:18—Simon (hearing) becomes Peter (rock)
   - Acts 13:9—Saul (asked) becomes Paul (little)

3. *Name Collage*
   Ask students to draw their names on construction paper. Make a collage of the names of the class and keep it up in the teaching area during the sessions. Or you might display the name tags made by the students at the beginning of the session.

4. *Name Quilt*
   Give each student a sheet of drawing paper. Divide each sheet into 3 inch squares. Using large bubble letters, have each student write his or her name, one letter per square, to fill up the sheet. Ask

them to colour the squares as they wish. Perhaps each letter "a" might be the same colour, and so on. Assemble the sheets to form a large group quilt.

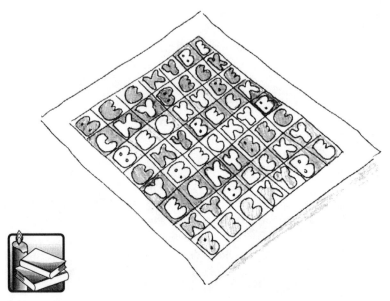

Literature

A Wind in the Door by Madeleine L'Engle. This novel describes the adventures of Meg Murry and her small brother Charles Wallace, as they battle evil both in galactic space and in the miniature world of the mitochondria in the bloodstream. The novel talks about "Naming."

Read the students the following excerpt:

> [The cherubim Proginoskes tells Meg that she is a Namer and she asks what a Namer does.] "When I was memorizing the names of the stars, part of the purpose was to help them each to be more particularly the particular star each one was supposed to be. That's basically a Namer's job. Maybe you're supposed to make earthlings feel more human" (ch. 4, p. 79).

1. Proginoskes asks Meg who makes her feel most like herself, and who makes her feel least like herself. Ask the students:
   How would you answer Proginoskes's question?
   Who makes you feel the most you?
   How do you think we can help others to be more completely themselves?

Waters by Edith Newlin Chase and Ron Broda. This picture book is full of wonderful illustrations done in paper sculpture. Read the book aloud to the class as a way of exploring the symbolism of water.

Visitor

1. Invite to your class an adult who was baptized in recent years. Ask this person to share with the class why they decided to be baptized and what it has meant to him or her.

2. Invite the parents of a baby soon to be baptized. Ask them to share with the students why is it important to them to have their child baptized.

Worship

1. Use the prayer for the gifts of the Spirit on page 160 of the *BAS*.

2. Other suggested prayers may be found in the *BAS* on page 863, 348, or 385.

3. Use the prayers for the Anglican Communion for today in the *Anglican Cycle of Prayer.*

4. In a circle, pray aloud for each student by name. Ask for God's blessing on their work and play during the coming week.

5. Use the music suggestions on page 39.

For Next Week: Look ahead to the next session. Are there any materials you want the students to bring? Are there any supplies that you need to acquire?

What have you learned about your students that will help you in your planning for the next session?

Remember to pray for each of your students by name during the week.

Theme Two
God

Introduction

Central to our Christian faith is the doctrine of revelation. It is our belief that God chooses to be revealed to us. We can come to know God; God is not completely hidden from us.

God is revealed to us in many ways. We see the work of God the Creator in the natural world around us. Its beauty and order and variety speak to us of the abundance and generosity of God's love. Through the Scriptures, God is revealed to us in human history—in the patriarchs and prophets and judges; in the events of the Exodus, the Exile, and the return; in the lives of the men and women and children that are recorded in the Bible.

God is revealed to us supremely in the life, death, and resurrection of Jesus. God is revealed to us in the lives of faithful men, women, and children—those of the great saints of Christian history and those of ordinary people in our own communities.

In all these many ways we come to understand God's plan for us and our world. This theme gives us a chance to explore who God is and what that might mean for us.

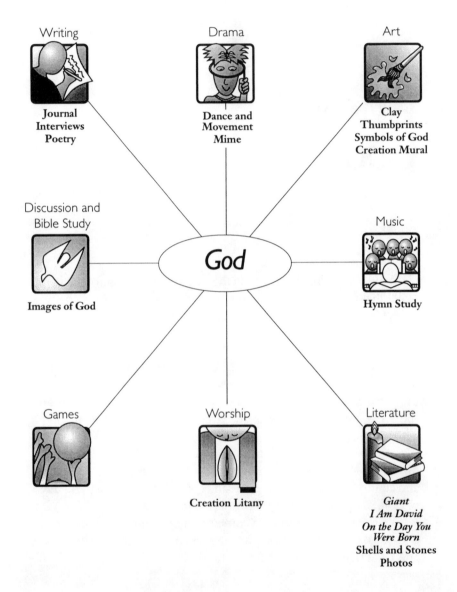

Writing

Journal
Interviews
Poetry

Drama

Dance and
Movement
Mime

Art

Clay
Thumbprints
Symbols of God
Creation Mural

Discussion and
Bible Study

Images of God

God

Music

Hymn Study

Games

Worship

Creation Litany

Literature

Giant
I Am David
On the Day You
Were Born
Shells and Stones
Photos

Literature

I Am David by Anne Holm. Here is a summary of the story:

Twelve-year-old David has spent all of his life in a concentration camp in Eastern Europe. He is given the chance to escape and is told to go to Italy and then north to Denmark. Because he has lived his whole life in the camp, he does not know anything about the world in which he finds himself. He does not know what food is safe to eat, what an orange is and how to eat it, or whom he can trust. This novel is the story of his adventures on the road to freedom.

Read aloud to the students the following passage:

When David loses [his compass], he cries aloud, "Oh God!" The sea was very deep under the rocks, and David knew he would never find the compass again. He sat for a long time staring at the place where it had disappeared. He was lost now. Now he would go round in circles and keep coming back to the same place. And they would find him.

He had had so little. Now he had nothing; nothing at all to safeguard his freedom.

"God!" he said softly. "Oh, God!"

He did not know why. It was what the men sometimes said in the camp when they were most in despair. But as for himself, he had no God.

And no compass either. Freedom was precious, and he had nothing to defend it with.

Then David decided that he must have a God: it might help. But which God should he choose? It was important to find the right one. If only he had listened more carefully to what the men had talked about in the camp! He had been interested only in learning new words. If he had asked more questions, he would have learned a lot more.

What gods did he know of? The one the Jews had made so many demands to in return for his help? And what had David to give? Nothing! And if you were not a Jew, perhaps you had no right to choose him. The God of the Catholics seemed to leave things to a woman called Mary. Not that David had anything against women, but as he knew so little about them it might be better to choose one who looked after things himself. Johannes should have taught him something about God. Instead, he had only told him about a man, also called David, who had lived a long time ago. David dug into his memory: when he thought hard he could recall many of the things Johannes had said. Was there not something about a god, too, in that story about David? Something in rather difficult words—he had always liked new words that were long and strange: he enjoyed finding out what they meant.

Suddenly it came back to him. That other David had said of his God, "He maketh me to lie down in green pastures. He leadeth me beside the still waters."

He was the one he would choose!

Clutching his orange tightly, he first looked round to make sure there was no one who could overhear him, and then said in a low voice, "God of the green pastures and the still waters, I am David and I choose you as my God! But you must please understand that I can't do anything for you, because I've always been in a wicked place where no one could think or learn or get to know anything, and I know nothing about what people ought to do for their God. But the David Johannes used to talk about knew that even if he couldn't see you, you were there and were stronger than any men. I pray you will help me so that *they* won't catch me again. Then perhaps I can gradually find out about you so that I can do something in return. And if you know where Johannes is now, will you please thank him for me for going with me to Salonica, and tell him that now I'm free I can think about him again. I am David. Amen."

Perhaps it was a mistake to say "amen" because that was what Catholics did, but David knew it was a holy word, and if you did not have an ending God would not know when you had finished your prayer.

He felt a sense of relief and added strength just as he had the morning he had determined to go on living. He was glad he had thought of it: a god would be a lot better than a compass ... though, of course, it would have been nice to have both (ch. 3, pp. 45–47).

Psalm 23. Look with your students at Psalm 23. Read the psalm aloud together to find out about the God of green pastures and still waters. Explain to the students that many of the psalms are attributed to David, the king of Israel. Ask the students to answer the following questions:

1. David decides to choose a God to follow. If you were choosing a God, what would that God be like?

2. There are many people in Canada today who know little about God, other than hearing God's name used as a swear word. What might you say to them about who God is?

3. In our culture, there is a lot of swearing. Is that okay? Why, or why not?

4. David finds himself in a desperate situation. Do you think that God intervenes to change things in our lives?

5. What questions would you like to ask God?

God the Creator

Literature

Read aloud to the class *On the Day You Were Born* by Debra Frasier. Here is a summary of the book:

> On the day of our births, the animals, the birds, all of creation prepares to welcome us and to say, "Welcome to the spinning world. Welcome to the green Earth. We are so glad you've come."

1. Have the students bring a picture of a place that is special to them and talk about why it is important for them. Ask them to list the things in the natural world which mean the most to them. Everyone's answers will be different. Discuss with the students: How do we make the world a welcoming place for all?

2. Look together at a book of photographs which show the variety and wonder in creation, such as *The Creation* by Ernest Haas. Use the photos as a starting point for discussion. You might want to bring other photos or posters to the classroom; for example, pictures taken by the Hubble space camera.

3. Tell the students: Each of you is created by God. What do you think God is most pleased with in you, God's creation? Talk about a part of you that you really like and why. "I like my eyes, my hands, my sense of humour." This might be a journal activity. Ask the students to write a paragraph or a poem.

4. Every part of God's creation is unique and special. So are we. Bring a jar of shells or stones to class. Have each student choose one and spend some time looking at it, touching it, smelling, tasting, getting to know the uniqueness of the object. Put the shells or stones back in the jar again. Have them try to recognize and pick out

their own. Read *Everybody Needs a Rock* by Byrd Baylor. He says that everybody needs a rock for a friend. The book sets out ten rules for finding your own special rock.

Art

Everyone's fingerprints are unique—no two fingerprints are alike. This allows detectives to use fingerprints as a way of identifying persons.

1. Provide a stamp pad and sheets of drawing paper. Ask each student to make several thumbprints on the paper and then add lines with pens and markers to create a picture. Ensure that handwashing facilities are nearby, or provide moist towelettes to help with the clean-up.

A good source of ideas is Ed Emberley's *Great Thumbprint Drawing Book*.

Images of God

Because we cannot see God, we use a variety of images or metaphors to describe what we believe God is like.

1. Ask the students to suggest an image or metaphor to describe themselves or a friend. Then ask them:
   When you think of God, what images come to mind?

Literature

Giant or Waiting for the Thursday Boat by Robert Munsch. Read this picture book aloud to the group. Provide a moment of silence at the end of the reading to allow the surprise ending to impact on the students.

Here is a summary of the story:

> The giant McKeon is angry with St Patrick because Patrick chased the snakes and elves and giants out of Ireland. When Patrick says that he was doing what God wanted, McKeon wants to fight with God, to pound God into applesauce. When he learns that God is coming on the Thursday boat, McKeon sits down by the shore to wait. In the first boat is a very small girl with a lot of small fish. She settles down beside McKeon to watch. Next comes a rich man, then a great soldier, but they are not God. McKeon picks up the little girl and jumps up to heaven but still cannot find God. Finally in the smallest house in heaven, McKeon finds all the snakes and elves and giants—and the little girl: "Then she started to laugh. She laughed till the mountains shook, rivers moved and stars changed directions. For a little girl she had an enormous laugh."

Ask the students these questions for discussion:

1. The psalms and other biblical texts portray God as a mighty ruler and warrior. What other images of God do we find in the Bible? Have the students brainstorm for a list of images they remember, or give them the following list of biblical verses to research. Assign a passage to each student, and ask them to identify what image of God is found there. Record their responses on newsprint.
   - shepherd (Psalm 23)
   - creator (Psalm 8, Job 38, 39, Genesis 1:1)
   - healer (Psalm 103:3)
   - protector (Psalm 104:5-9; 28:7)
   - mighty Saviour (Deuteronomy 32:18)
   - father (Matthew 6:9)
   - King of the earth (Daniel 2:47)
   - potter (Jeremiah 18:1–11)
   - husband (Hosea 2:2)
   - strengthener (Isaiah 40:28)
   - judge (Genesis 18:25, Proverbs 3:11)
   - rock (2 Samuel 22:3).

2. In *Giant*, God comes to the giant in the form of a little girl. The church is beginning to explore the use of both masculine and feminine images for God. Ask the students:
   What do you think of this?

   Some feminine images for God are found in these verses:
   - mother hen (Matthew 23:27; Luke 13:34)
   - mother eagle (Deut 32:11,12, Job 39)
   - woman seeking coin (Luke 15:8-10)
   - God as mother (Isaiah 42:14; Acts 17:26,28; Deut 32:18)
   - midwife (Isaiah 66:9, Psalm 22:9,10)
   - Dame Wisdom (Wisdom of Solomon 8:4)
   - mother bear (Hosea 13:8)
   - bakerwoman (Matthew 13:33).

   Again, give the students verses to look up. List the images for God on newsprint.

3. In the book, God came to the giant in a very unexpected way. In the Bible, when the people of Israel were expecting God to send a king, God sent the infant Son instead. Today, God comes to us in unexpected ways. Ask the students:

   How do we see God at work in the world today?

   Can you think of any unexpected ways in which God has come to you?

4. Some have criticized this book because the giant becomes angry with God and threatens to pound God into applesauce. Ask:

   Is it all right to be angry with God?

   Has this ever happened to you?

Sometimes the psalmist seems to be angry with God, to question why God seems to be absent from his life. Look with the students at the following psalms: 10:1; 13:1,2; 22:1,2; 74:1.

Music

1. In *The Magician's Nephew* by C. S. Lewis, Aslan the lion (who is the figure of Jesus) creates the world of Narnia by singing. Read chapter 8 (p. 93ff) and chapter 9 of this story aloud to the students with the accompaniment of taped music, perhaps part of *The Planets Suite* by Gustav Holst, *And God Created Great Whales* by Alan Hovhaness, or tapes of sounds from nature.

2. One of our hymns, "God who Gives to Life its Beauty," includes the phrase, "God who names us co-creators." Ask the students:

   What might this phrase mean?

   In what ways might human beings be "co-creators" with God?

3. Give each student a hymn book and ask them to find as many different images of God in hymns as they can. For instance, they

might discover "The King of Love My Shepherd Is"; "The Lord's My Shepherd"; "King of Glory."

4. A more recent hymn is "Bring Many Names" by Brian Wren. See the text on page 60, and list each image for God on a sheet. Ask the students what each image suggests to them about who God is and what God is like.

Dance and Movement

If dance activities do not come easily to you, consider inviting someone else from the congregation to come in and assist you with these activities. You may have dance students in your group who would be pleased to share their talent with the class.

1. As a warm-up, mime the movement from darkness to light in creation. Ask the students to curl themselves up into a very small ball, hidden in the darkness. Then have them slowly stretch up tall as the light dawns and awakens them to life.

2. Read aloud this passage about the birth of a star from *A Wind in the Door* by Madeleine L'Engle:

> Meg looked about. Ahead of her was a tremendous rhythmic swirl of wind and flame, but it was wind and flame quite different from the cherubim's; this was a dance, a dance ordered and graceful, and yet giving an impression of complete and utter freedom, of ineffable joy. As the dance progressed, the movement accelerated and the pattern became clearer, closer, wind and fire moving together, and there was joy, and song, melody soaring, gathering together as wind and fire united.
>
> And then wind, flame, dance, song, cohered in a great swirling, leaping, dancing, single sphere.

Meg heard Mr. Jenkins's incredulous, "What was that?"
Blajeny replied, "The birth of a star" (ch. 8, p. 148).

Create a dance or series of movements which might illustrate the birth of a star, of a tree, of the animals. You may wish to use taped music as accompaniment.

Art

1. Read aloud Genesis 1 or 2. Record on newsprint the order in which things were created, and discuss with the students any questions they may have about these stories. Some very good questions may be raised, leading to a thoughtful discussion. Ask the students to plan a mural showing the events of the creation story and create it on a large sheet of paper. Play some background music, classical or sounds of nature, as the class works.

2. There are many different images of God in art. The Jewish religion prohibits the use of God's name and the drawing of any pictures or images of God. Orthodox Christians use ikons with stylized representations of the three Persons of God and the saints. In art and church decoration, there are a number of traditional symbols for God. The triangle and the three leaves or "trefoil" remind us of God's three-fold nature. The circle, without beginning and end, is another symbol for God. Sometimes God the creator is portrayed by the hand and sometimes by the all-seeing eye. Have the students look in the church for these symbols. Ask them to brainstorm for responses to "What is God like?" and then create a symbol for God.

3. Read aloud once again *On the Day You Were Born*. Have the students respond to the story using finger paints or oil pastels. Talk about the variety of creation.

4. One of the biblical images for God is as the potter shaping us, God's creation. In Genesis 2:7, we read that God formed us of the dust of the earth. In Jeremiah 18:1–11, God tells Israel, "I am the potter." Bring some clay to class and have your students share in the creative process. Teaching supply stores sell self-hardening clay, which is inexpensive and does not need to be fired. *The Potter* by Jacolyn Caton or *When Clay Sings* by Byrd Baylor would be good books to read aloud to the class as they work.

Poetry

1. Read aloud the poem "Bakerwoman God" on page 61. Ask the students:
   What is this author trying to express about God in her poem?

2. Ask the students to brainstorm for images of God. Then ask them to write their own poem about God in their journal.

3. Here are some ideas to help students get started writing poetry. Remind them that a poem does not have to rhyme, nor does it have to have lines of the same length or metre.
   • Write a group poem, with each student contributing one line.
   • Ask the students to brainstorm for a list of metaphors:
     God is...
     Love is...

4. Ask each student to complete the following phrases and contribute an idea:
   • If I ruled the world...
   • I wish...
   • I want to ask God...
   • I think about God when...

Group poems can be displayed on newsprint, or students might prefer to write a poem in their journal. They may choose to share it with the class, or they may want to keep it private.

Writing

Arrange for students to interview some members of the congregation about their experience of God or their ideas about God. With their consent, include these in a newsletter to be shared with the class and with others.

Worship

1. In your worship, use prayers which speak of God's work of creation. A good collection is *Earth Prayers* by Elizabeth Roberts and Elias Amidon. Here are some suggestions from *The Book of Alternative Services*:
   - #12, page 132
   - page 845
   - page 833
   - page 712.

2. Brainstorm with your students for ideas for a litany that gives thanks for the goodness of creation. Record the litany on newsprint for use as part of your worship, or ask each student to think of one petition and share it in the circle as part of the concluding worship.

3. Use one of the hymns studied earlier, or together sing a hymn which praises God for the created world.

For Next Week: Look ahead to the next session. Is there anything your students need to bring? Are there any supplies you need to acquire?

What have you learned from this week's session which will help you to plan for next week?

Remember to pray for your students during the week. What is going on in your church or community which affects their lives?

Bring Many Names

Bring many names, beautiful and good,
celebrate, in parable and story,
holiness in glory, living, loving God.
Hail and Hosanna! bring many names!

Strong mother God, working night and day,
planning all the wonders of creation,
setting each equation, genius at play:
Hail and Hosanna, strong mother God!

Warm father God, hugging every child,
feeling all the strains of human living,
caring and forgiving till we're reconciled:
Hail and Hosanna, warm father God!

Old, aching God, grey with endless care,
calmly piercing evil's new disguises,
glad of good surprises, wiser than despair:
Hail and Hosanna, old, aching God!

Young, growing God, eager, on the move,
seeing all, and fretting at our blindness,
crying out for justice, giving all you have:
Hail and Hosanna, young, growing God!

Great, living God, never fully known,
joyful darkness far beyond our seeing,
closer yet than breathing, everlasting home:
Hail and Hosanna, great, living God!

—Words: Brian Wren

Bakerwoman God

Bakerwoman God,
I am your living bread.
Strong, brown Bakerwoman God,
I am your low, soft, and being-shaped loaf.
I am your rising
bread, well-kneaded
by some divine and knotty
pair of knuckles,
by your warm earth hands.
I am bread well-kneaded.

Put me in fire, Bakerwoman God,
put me in your own bright fire.

I am warm, warm as you from fire.
I am white and gold, soft and hard,
brown and round.
I am so warm from fire.

Break me, Bakerwoman God!
I am broken under your caring Word.
Drop me in your special juice in pieces.
Drop me in your blood.
Drunken me in the great red flood.
Self-giving chalice, swallow me.
My skin shines in the divine wine.
My face is cup-covered and I drown.

I fall up
in a red pool
in a gold world
where your warm
sunskin hand is there
to catch and hold me.
Bakerwoman God, remake me.

—Allah Bozarth-Campbell, *Womanpriest* (pp. 217–218).

Theme Three

Jesus

Introduction

As Christians, we believe that God is revealed supremely in Jesus, who became fully human and lived and died as one of us.

In John 1:1, Jesus is called the Word of God. As the Word, Jesus existed from the beginning. The Word was the agent of creation— "through him all things were made" (Nicene Creed).

Jesus became incarnate, took on flesh and was fully human, to share our earthly life. He came to reveal God's love and to show that love is stronger than evil and death. By his willingness to suffer and to die for all humankind, Jesus showed the depths of God's love for us, even when we reject that love. God raised Jesus from the dead and conquered the power of sin and death.

Jesus ascended to heaven but promised his followers that God the Holy Spirit would be with them to strengthen and empower them to serve God and other people.

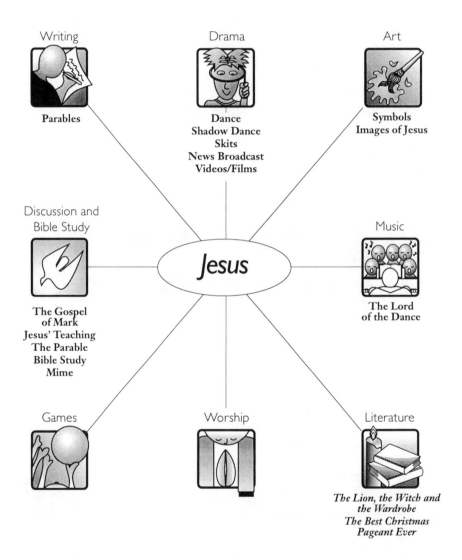

Writing

Parables

Drama

Dance
Shadow Dance
Skits
News Broadcast
Videos/Films

Art

Symbols
Images of Jesus

Discussion and
Bible Study

The Gospel
of Mark
Jesus' Teaching
The Parable
Bible Study
Mime

Jesus

Music

The Lord
of the Dance

Games

Worship

Literature

The Lion, the Witch and
the Wardrobe
The Best Christmas
Pageant Ever

Bible

Here are several activities to help students explore the life of Jesus.

1. Ask the students to read the Gospel of Mark. This should take about twenty to thirty minutes. Students could take turns reading the Gospel aloud. This is the earliest and shortest of the Gospels—just sixteen chapters. Reading it in its entirety will help the students get an overview of the life of Jesus.

2. On a time line, trace the events of Jesus' life as recorded in Mark's Gospel.

3. Take a tour of the windows and other decorations in the church to view the symbols of the life, death, and resurrection of Jesus. Good books containing explanations of religious symbols are *Saints, Signs and Symbols* by W. Ellwood Post and *Symbols of Church Seasons and Days* by John Bradner.

Music and Dance

If you feel that you need help with these activities, ask someone in the congregation or community to assist you.

1. Sing together the hymn "Lord of the Dance" (The Hymn Book, #106).

Background

Verse 1:   Jesus as God exists before the Creation and, as the Word, brings the Creation to birth; the Incarnation—God enters our world in human form.

Verse 2:   Conflict arises as Jesus' ministry and teaching begins to challenge the religious establishment; the call to the disciples to follow Jesus.

Verse 3:   Jesus' ministry of healing; the crucifixion—the response of some to Jesus' call to wholeness of life.

Verse 4:   Jesus' death and the promise of everlasting life.

Verse 5:   The Resurrection—new life for all when we live in Christ.

Ask the students what events in Jesus' life each verse describes. In the hymn, Jesus is given to say, "I am the dance and I still go on." Ask the students in what ways the dance is an image of the church.

2. Invite a dancer to come and share some ideas about liturgical dance with the class. He or she might help the class create movements that would express the meaning of this hymn or another part of the liturgy.

3. The dance suggests a number of images to us. Ask the students: What do you think of when you think of "the dance?"

Brainstorm for ideas. Here are some possible responses you may receive:
• dance has a pattern, order
• it has a structure, yet is flexible
• it is seldom solitary; it usually involves partners or a troupe
• the number of dancers may be large or small
• leadership changes from time to time
• it is unending
• it may tell a story
• dance expresses a feeling
• it expresses a rhythm
• it comforts
• it energizes.

Some people cannot dance with their bodies. Ask the students how the image of the dance can include these persons as well and if there are other ways of dancing than by moving your feet.

4. Imagine that you are someone's shadow. The shadow follows the movements of the leader. Ask one student to stand facing the class and make slow, dance-like movements. Ask the class to mirror these movements. Change the leadership from time to time. Or you might ask the class to stand in a line. Have the leader begin dancing slowly, while each person in the line shadows the leader. The person at the back of the line then advances and becomes the next leader.

   Use slow music, such as Pachelbel's "Canon"; "Gymnopedies" by Erik Satie; the soundtrack from the movie *Chariots of Fire*.

Art

1. Bring a variety of pictures of Jesus to class. Christmas cards are a good source, as well as Bible story books and curriculum materials. Ask the students to bring pictures too. Jesus has been depicted in many different ways in many different cultures. Here are some suggestions for a variety of pictures:
   • crucifix—the suffering Christ
   • Christus Rex—Christ triumphant in priestly robes
   • Jesus as pictured by other races and cultures
   • the birth of Jesus
   • laughing Jesus
   • sorrowful Jesus
   • Jesus with children.

2. Frederick Buechner's *The Faces of Jesus* is an excellent additional resource, as well as William Kurelek's *A Northern Nativity*, which pictures the birth of Jesus set in western and northern Canada. Ask the students:

If Jesus were born in your town, where might he live? What kind of family might he have?

Videos/Films

There are many videos and films which depict the life of Jesus. Check to see how suitable these are for the average age of your group members.

Jesus Christ Superstar and *Godspell* are two musical versions. *The Cottonpatch Gospel* is a re-telling of the gospel in the speech patterns of the southern United States.

Church resource centres carry many filmstrips and videos of biblical stories.

Literature

Jesus' Birth

The Best Christmas Pageant Ever by Barbara Robinson. This is a good read-aloud book for all ages. You might want to make time to read it aloud to the class. Here is a summary of the story:

> The Herdmans, a dreadful bunch of children who swear and smoke and terrorize others, take over the main roles in the church Christmas pageant because of the promise of free refreshments. They hear the Christmas story for the first time and are astonished by what they hear.

Read aloud the following excerpt:

> "What's that?" they would yell whenever they didn't understand the language, and when Mother read about

there being no room at the inn, Imogene's jaw dropped and she sat up in her seat.

"My God!" she said. "Not even for Jesus?"

I saw Alice purse her lips together so I knew that was something else Mrs. Wendleken would hear about—swearing in the church.

"Well, now, after all," Mother explained, "nobody knew the baby was going to turn out to be Jesus."

"You said Mary knew," Ralph said. "Why didn't she tell them?"

"*I* would have told them!" Imogene put in. "Boy, would I have told them! What was the matter with Joseph that he didn't tell them? Her pregnant and everything," she grumbled.

"What was that they laid the baby in?" Leroy said. "That manger ... is that like a bed? Why would they have a bed in the barn?"

"That's just the point," Mother said. "They *didn't* have a bed in the barn, so Mary and Joseph had to use whatever there was. What would you do if you had a new baby and no bed to put the baby in?"

"We put Gladys in a bureau drawer," Imogene volunteered.

"Well, there you are," Mother said, blinking a little. "You didn't have a bed for Gladys so you had to use something else."

"Oh, we had a bed," Ralph said, "only Ollie was still in it and he wouldn't get out. He didn't like Gladys." He elbowed Ollie. "Remember how you didn't like Gladys?"

I thought that was pretty smart of Ollie, not to like Gladys right off the bat.

"*Anyway,*" Mother said, "Mary and Joseph used the manger. A manger is a large wooden feeding trough for animals."

"What were the wadded-up clothes?" Claude wanted to know.

"The what?" Mother said.

"You read about it—'she wrapped him in wadded-up clothes.'"

"*Swaddling* clothes." Mother sighed. "Long ago, people used to wrap their babies very tightly in big pieces of material, so they couldn't move around. It made the babies feel cozy and comfortable."

I thought it probably just made the babies mad. Till then, I didn't know what swaddling clothes were either, and they sounded terrible, so I wasn't too surprised when Imogene got all excited about that.

"You mean they tied him up and put him in a feedbox?" she said. "Where was the Child Welfare?"

The Child Welfare was always checking up on the Herdmans. I'll bet if the Child Welfare had ever found Gladys all tied up in a bureau drawer they would have done something about it.

"And, lo, the Angel of the Lord came upon them," Mother went on, "and the glory of the Lord shone round about them, and—"

"Shazam!" Gladys yelled, flinging her arms out and smacking the kid next to her.

"What?" Mother said. Mother never read "Amazing Comics."

"Out of the black night with horrible vengeance, the Mighty Marvo—"

"I don't know what you're talking about, Gladys," Mother said. "This is the Angel of the Lord who comes to the shepherd in the fields, and—"

"Out of nowhere, right?" Gladys said. "In the black night, right?"

"Well..." Mother looked unhappy. "In a way."

So Gladys sat back down, looking very satisfied, as if this was at least one part of the Christmas story that made sense to her (ch. 4, pp. 43–45).

1. The Christmas story is so familiar to us. Ask the students:
   Which parts of the story do the Herdmans notice when it is
     read to them?

2. Read aloud to the students the birth narratives (Luke, Matthew).
   Ask them:
   What is most surprising to you in this story?

3. How do other cultures look at the Christmas story? In Australia
   and New Zealand, Christmas comes in the middle of summer.
   They sing the traditional carols which describe snow and winter,
   but they have also written carols describing their own Christmas
   setting. Here is one example to share with the students:

> Carol our Christmas,
> an upside down Christmas;
> snow is not falling and
> trees are not bare.
> Carol the summer, and
> welcome the Christ Child,
> warm in our sunshine and
> sweetness of air.
> Sing of the gold and the
> green and the sparkle,
> water and river and lure
> of the beach.
> Sing of the happiness
> of open spaces,
> sing a nativity summer
> can reach!

—Shirley Erena Murray

4. Ask the students to find out how other cultures re-tell the Christmas story. Public and school libraries will offer useful material.

Jesus' Death and Resurrection

The Lion, the Witch and the Wardrobe by C. S. Lewis. Here is a summary of the story:

> In this book, Jesus is represented by Aslan, the lion.
> The child Edmund betrays Narnia, and Aslan voluntarily
> pays the penalty which the White Witch has demanded.
> Aslan is killed and then raised to new life.

1. Read aloud to the students the death and resurrection scenes in chapters 14 and 15. Ask them:
   What are your reactions to these scenes?
   Does this help you to see anything about Jesus' death in a new way?

This book is available on video, so you might consider scheduling a session to allow the group to see it.

Jesus' Teaching

1. Discussion
   Ask your students to think of a person who is a good teacher. Ask them what makes a good teacher. Share other stories of good teachers, and ask the students:
   Why do we think that teachers should be an example for others?
   What made Jesus a good teacher?
   What are some of the ways in which he taught? (parables, sayings, actions, the example of his life)

2. The Parable

One method of teaching which Jesus used was the parable. The parable is a story which is designed to illustrate one point. It is not an allegory, in which every detail of the story has a hidden significance, but it is a vivid example, usually drawn from everyday experience, which communicates a major teaching. Look at some examples from the Gospels:

• the Mustard Seed (Mark 4:30–32)
• the Leaven (Luke 13:20–21)
• the Hidden Treasure (Matthew 13:44–46).

3. One of the modern parables often quoted is the story of the Canada geese. When the geese fly in a V-formation, one goose serves as the leader, breaking a path through the wind for the following flock. As the lead goose tires, another moves forward and takes its place as leader. And so leadership and responsibility are shared as the flock travels.

Share with your students one or two of the biblical parables, and then tell them the story of the Canada geese. Have them brainstorm for ideas about what would make a good parable and then write their own parables to share with the class. These might form part of a newsletter or display.

Jesus' Disciples

The following activities will give the students the opportunity to do research, using the Bible and other materials. Help the students to discover where information can be found—material in church and public libraries; the calendar in the *BAS* and *BCP*; dictionaries of saints.

1. Read together the story of the call of some of the disciples: Mark 1:16–20; Luke 5:27; John 1:40–51. On newsprint, compare the lists of disciples from Matthew 10:2–4, Mark 3:16–19, Luke 6:14–

16. Assign to each student the name of a disciple and ask them to find out all they can about this person. For example, what is the symbol that represents the disciple? When is the feast day? Ask the students:

What happened to Judas, and who replaced him in the Twelve? (Acts 1:26).

Who were the women who were part of the band of people who travelled with Jesus? (Mary and Martha, Mary Magdalene, Joanna, and the women who came to the tomb).

What can you find out about women and their place among Jesus' followers?

The books *WomanWord*, *WomanWitness*, and *WomanWisdom* by Miriam Therese Winter are excellent resources for information about little-known women of the Bible.

2. Discussion

In our society we look up to sports heroes and often view them as examples to follow. Ask the students if this is a good idea. Have them compare and contrast the disciples and a sports team. Ask:

Did the disciples have particular roles in the group?

How did they get along?

How did Jesus serve as their captain?

Drama

1. Ask the students to develop a news broadcast in which they cover the events of Christmas or of Holy Week. There is plenty of contrasting emotions in these stories, from darkness and discouragement to the excitement of new life. Choose announcers and reporters from the group and allow them time to prepare a script.

2. Have the students create skits based on episodes in the life and teaching of Jesus, and then perform them for the group. Here are some suggestions:
   - The good Samaritan (Luke 10:25–37)
   - The prodigal son (Luke 15:11–32)
   - The call of the disciples (Luke 5:1–11, 27–32)
   - The feeding of the 5000 (Matthew 14:13–21).

The Spirit

God the Holy Spirit came to the disciples at Pentecost to empower them to tell others the good news of Jesus. The Spirit continues to act today, to teach us, to encourage us, to strengthen us to follow Jesus.

1. Read aloud the Pentecost story in Acts 2:1–13. Have one student read the story aloud and ask the others to make sound effects. Ask the students:
   How might those present have felt?
   What sounds might you hear during the events of the story?

2. The fruits of the Spirit are the results of God's action in our lives. Read aloud Galatians 5:22 and list the gifts as written: love, joy, peace, patience, kindness, goodness, fidelity, gentleness, self-control. Talk with the students about what these words mean. Ask:
   How do we show these qualities in everyday life?

Give each student a word to illustrate. Have them create and perform skits or use mime to illustrate each characteristic.

Worship

1. Sing the hymn "Lord of the Dance."

2. Together, say the prayer of St Richard of Chichester:

> O holy Jesus,
>
> Most merciful redeemer, friend and brother,
>
> May we see thee more clearly,
>
> Love thee more dearly
>
> And follow thee more nearly
>
> Day by Day. Amen.

3. Say together the Lord's Prayer, the prayer which Jesus taught his disciples.

For next week: What materials do you need for next week's class? Is there anything that the students need to bring?

What have you learned from your students to help you to plan for the next session? What is going on in the students' lives that will have an impact on your time together?

Remember to pray for your students during the coming week.

Theme Four
The Church

Introduction

Jesus brought his followers together into a community, forming a group who met together regularly to worship God, to study, to share as widely as possible the good news of God's love, and to care for each other and the wider society in which they lived. The Holy Spirit strengthens and empowers the church for its mission.

By baptism, we become members of the community of the church. Children, adolescents, adults, the elderly—all are full members of the church. We come together regularly to worship God and to share in the Eucharist, the family meal.

Together we learn and study so that we may grow in our understanding of the faith. As Anglicans, we have certain traditions and customs that define our family life. We are part of a Canadian family and also part of a worldwide Anglican family. Learning more about the Anglican family and its traditions is an important part of this theme.

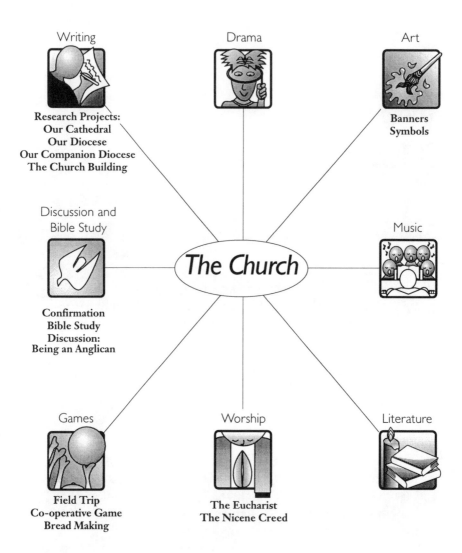

Writing

Research Projects:
Our Cathedral
Our Diocese
Our Companion Diocese
The Church Building

Drama

Art

Banners
Symbols

Discussion and
Bible Study

Music

The Church

Confirmation
Bible Study
Discussion:
Being an Anglican

Games

Worship

Literature

Field Trip
Co-operative Game
Bread Making

The Eucharist
The Nicene Creed

What Does It Mean To Be an Anglican?

Anglicans are members of a worldwide family of churches, known as the Anglican Communion. There are thirty-seven member churches or "provinces"; The Anglican Church of Canada is a province. The Episcopal Church in the United States, the Church of England, the Church of the Province of Southern Africa, the Nippon Sei Ko Kai, (the Holy Catholic Church in Japan)—all are provinces of the Anglican Communion. All these churches trace their descent from the Church of England, from which we inherited the Prayer Book and forms of worship, our customs and traditions, our form of government in which the bishop has the authority within the diocese, and a characteristic way of doing theology. (See *This Anglican Church of Ours* [Wood Lake Books, 1995] or *Meet the Family* [Anglican Book Centre and Wood Lake Books, 1996] for more information about Anglican theology and customs.)

A map which shows the partner churches of the Anglican Communion is available through the World Mission (Partnerships) department of the Anglican Church of Canada. Many parishes have a copy of the map displayed in the church or hall. Use the map to show your students where Anglicans are found worldwide. The *Anglican Cycle of Prayer* is published each year by Forward Movement Publications. Each parish should have a copy of this prayer cycle to help in preparing the intercessions for each Sunday. Use the background notes following each intercession and share this information with your students. These may be photocopied.

The appendix to this volume, "What Does It Mean To Be an Anglican?", may be copied and given to each student. You might hand it out before the class to allow the students time to read the material and to come up with questions.

Research Projects

What follows are a number of research projects which might be assigned to the students. Begin by handing out copies of the Worksheet "Research Projects," on page 81. Discuss the projects with the class and let each person choose a topic they would like to research. Ask them to report back to the class at the next session. Direct them to sources of information, such as the parish clergy, the diocesan office, the national church newspaper, *The Anglican Journal*, or the diocesan newspaper.

You will need to help the students to develop the questions they would like to ask the bishop for Research Project number 3, "Our Bishop." It would be good to have some or all of the class interview the bishop, if possible. If not, the diocesan office or the diocesan newspaper would be a good source for photos and information.

Display the completed projects for the whole parish to see, or display them at a deanery or diocesan event. You might like to share your research with people in your companion diocese.

Worksheet 6: *Research Projects*

1. *Companion Dioceses*

Many dioceses in Canada have a "companion diocese," a diocese in another part of the Anglican Communion with which they have a particular link. People from one diocese visit the other from time to time, and newspapers and other information are exchanged. Does your diocese have a companion diocese? What is its name? Where is it located? Find out more about it and report to the group. If you can locate maps or pictures, these could be used to show something of the life of that diocese. Find the section of the *Anglican Cycle of Prayer* where we remember your companion diocese. What are the concerns for which they have asked our prayers?

2. *Our Diocese*

How did our diocese get its name? How big is it, and what are its boundaries? What are some of the highlights of its history? How many members are in the diocese? How many parishes? Call the diocesan office for information about the diocese. They may have an information sheet which gives many of the details you are looking for. *The Anglican Church Directory*, found in many parish offices, gives statistical information about all dioceses in Canada. There may be a history of the diocese in book form. The diocesan newspaper is another source. Use a map to show the location and boundaries of the diocese, and bring any pictures illustrating diocesan history.

3. *Our Bishop*

What is our bishop's name? How long has he or she been a bishop? Where does the bishop live? What is the work of a bishop?

4. *Our Ministry and Clergy*

Who is the Archdeacon? The regional dean? The dean of the cathedral? What is their work? See the handout "What Does It Mean To Be an Anglican?" for some definitions. Who is the rector/other clergy/

ministry team? What work do they do? What is the vestry/parish council?

5. *Our Cathedral*

What is its name? When was it built? Who is the dean? Why is the cathedral important? How is it part of our life as members of the diocese? David Macaulay has written a book, *Cathedral*, which shows how a mediaeval cathedral was built. He has also produced an excellent video with the same title.

6. *Our Parish*

What is its name? When was the church built? What can you find out about the history of the congregation? Many communities have published local history books which include a history of the church. To which saint is the church dedicated? What can you find out about that saint?

Visits

1. Tour the church building with the students, looking at the architecture, the furniture, the symbols. Ask the students:
   For what saint is the church named?
   What other saints are pictured in the windows?

2. Have the students look for cross shapes in the church. Ask:
   How many can you find?
   What different types of crosses are there?

3. Have the students write a tour guide to your church, or have them act as tour guides for others at a parish event.

4. With your students, visit
   - other churches in your town
   - the cathedral
   - the churches of other denominations in town.

The book *What It Feels Like to Be a Building* by Forrest Wilson provides an interesting look at architecture and how buildings are designed.

Co-operative Game

One of the images we use to describe the church is the Body of Christ. By our baptism, we are all members of that body, of which Christ is the head. Here is a game which uses the image of the body.

Divide the class into groups of five, or, with a group of six or seven, play the game twice with different participants. Give each person in the group a label to show that they are either "eyes," "ears," "hands," "feet," or "mouth." Each part of the body except the "eyes" should be blindfolded. The whole group then tries to perform as one body a simple task assigned by you. Whisper the task to the "ears" who will then whisper it to the "mouth." The "mouth" then tells the group what to do.

For example, place a chocolate bar on a table at the other end of the room. Ask the "body," moved by the "feet" and guided by the "eyes," to move to the chocolate bar. The "hands" guided by the "eyes" will then open the wrapper and feed the "mouth." The body then has to throw the wrapper in the garbage can at the other end of the room.

Repeat the exercise, or similar tasks, several times. Discuss it with the students. Ask:

What was it like to be part of the group?

Was it easy to co-operate?

Did anyone opt out?

What does this tell us about how the body works?

Exploring the Eucharist

The Eucharist is one of the sacraments of the church. A sacrament is defined in the Catechism (*BCP*, page 550) as "an outward and visible sign of an inward and spiritual grace." God's grace comes to us through things that we can see and touch and taste. In the Eucharist, God comes to us in the bread and the wine. We can touch and taste them, yet they convey to us the invisible and intangible riches of spiritual grace. We bring the bread and wine, which represent our daily life and work. We receive back again the bread and wine, now transformed by God's Spirit into vehicles for sharing God's love with us.

1. Have the students brainstorm for all the names by which the Eucharist is known: the Eucharist, the Lord's Supper, the Holy Com-

munion, the Mass. Ask them what the significance is of each of these names.

The Eucharist—a Greek word meaning "Thanksgiving." We give thanks to God for God's great gift of new life through Christ's life, death, and resurrection.

The Lord's Supper—this is the Christian family meal, instituted by Jesus at the Last Supper which he shared with his disciples. We meet together to follow Jesus' command, "Do this in remembrance of me."

The Holy Communion—a solemn event which brings us closer to God and to each other. We share this sacrament with each other in community.

The Mass—This name comes from the final words of the traditional Latin text, *Ite, missa est;* "Go, you have been sent." We come to the Eucharist to be strengthened for carrying out Christ's mission in the world. We are fed in order that we can go out and do the work of mission in the world. We use this name particularly at Christmas, the "Christ Mass."

2. There are many meanings of the Eucharist—the forgiveness of our sins, the remembrance of Christ's death and resurrection, thanksgiving, a feast, a family meal, a way in which we experience the presence of God. Ask:
   How is the Eucharist similar to and different from a family meal?

3. Have the students recall some special meals that they have been a part of. Discuss with them:
   What made them memorable for you?
   What does it mean to share a meal with someone?

4. Have the students look up the following biblical passages:
   • Matthew 16:32–38 (Jesus feeds the 4,000)
   • Matthew 26:17–30 (The Last Supper)
   • Mark 2:15–16 (Jesus eats with sinners)

- Mark 6:39–44 (Jesus feeds the 5,000)
- Luke 14: 1, 12–14 (Jesus eats with a Pharisee)
- Luke 19:1–10 (Jesus eats with Zacchaeus)
- Luke 7:36–50 (The anointing of Jesus' feet)
- John 2:1–11 (The wedding at Cana)
- John 12:1–3 (Jesus eats at the home of Martha and Mary)
- John 21:9–14 (Jesus eats with his friends after his resurrection).

Discuss with the students the meals that Jesus took part in. Ask:
What was the occasion?
Who was there?
What did Jesus say and do? What do you think you would
    have felt like if you had been there?
Are there aspects of the Eucharist meal which are like other
    meals, perhaps meals shared with your family, or meals at
    school?

5. We believe that God has created the world, and that material things
   are vehicles through which God's grace comes to us. Anglicans
   believe in the importance of using all our senses in worship. Our
   services use colour, music, symbols, art, the scent of flowers and
   sometimes incense, the taste of the bread and wine, the touching
   of hands at the passing of the peace, the changing of posture from
   sitting to kneeling to standing.
      Have the students brainstorm for a list of ways in which we use
   our senses in worship. Talk with the class about gestures in worship, such as the passing of the Peace, the sign of cross. Think of
   those things which appeal to our sense of sight, touch, taste, smell,
   hearing.

A Walk through the Eucharist
Divide the students into groups and ask them to answer the following questions on the Worksheet (page 87) using the *BAS*. You may
assign one section of the service to each group, or, with a small class,
you might ask the whole group to work through all the sections of
the service. You may wish to adapt these questions to the traditional
language service in the *BAS* or to the service in the *BCP*. The questions are designed to help the students explore the pattern of the
service and to find their way around the *BAS*.

Worksheet 7: *The Eucharist*

The Gathering (pp. 185–187)

1. We use the same gathering prayers each Sunday except during the season of...

2. At which seasons do we use the hymn "Glory to God"?

3. When do we use the Kyrie or Trisagion?

4. What is a Collect?

The Proclamation of the Word (pp. 187–192)

1. From which parts of the Bible do we read?

2. What are the two Creeds which we use?

3. Where do we find suggestions for the Prayers of the People?

4. What are we doing in the Confession and Absolution?

5. What happens at the Peace?

The Celebration of the Eucharist (pp. 192–214)

1. What happens at the Offertory?

2. Why do we give money?

3. How many eucharistic prayers are there?

4. What prayer do we say at the end of the eucharistic prayer?

5. What happens next? (pp. 212–213)

After Communion

1. What happens after Communion?

Talk with the students about eucharistic customs in your own parish. Some may already be receiving Communion. Others may be preparing for their First Communion.

You may wish to take some time at the main Sunday Eucharist, when the students are present, and explain what is happening during each part of the liturgy. This could be a learning experience for the whole congregation. An Instructed Eucharist could be done by the presider or one of the clergy, or a lay person could introduce each section of the Eucharist by reading the commentary from the lectern.

Diane Brooks is the author of an interesting Canadian picture book called *Passing the Peace*. This is a counting book of the numbers one through ten in English, French, Inuktitut, and Inuinnagtun. Using the Inuit technique of appliqué, the pictures show a circle of parka-clad figures holding hands. As each number is counted, the circle of light spreads from one figure to another. The author writes that the book "grew out of two things: my desire to make an elementary counting book for a new niece, and my love of the Christian theme of passing the Lord's peace through touch." You might read this book aloud to the class after you have discussed with them the meaning of passing the peace.

Memory Work

The Nicene Creed is used during the Eucharist. Ask the class to memorize it.

Prayer

The students may wish to memorize this Canadian prayer for the church (*BAS*, p. 676, #2):

> Draw your church together, O Lord,
>
> into one great company of disciples,
>
> together following our Lord Jesus Christ
>
> into every walk of life,
>
> together serving him in his mission to the world,
>
> and together witnessing to his love
>
> on every continent and island.
>
> Amen.

Music

1. Together with the students, learn some of the hymns to be used at the confirmation service. The class might form a choir and sing one of the hymns as an anthem.

2. Learn a communion hymn, such as "Let Us Break Bread Together."

3. "La Cathédrale Engloutie," one of the Preludes by Debussy, tells the story of the old cathedral of Ys. The cathedral is now under the sea ("drowned," as in the title). On clear days, when the sea is transparent, the cathedral rises from the waters, with its bells tolling and priests chanting. The music expresses its rise and slow return to the depths. Play this piece as your students work on an art or writing project.

Group Activity

With the students, bake the bread to be used at confirmation Eucharist. There are many recipes for altar bread; one source is *Best Recipes This Side of Heaven*. Here is a recipe from that book, contributed by St Mark's Church, Port Hope, Ont.

> Mix in a large bowl:
> 4 cups whole wheat flour
> 4 tsp. baking powder
> 2 tsp. salt
>
> In a smaller bowl, mix:
> 1/2 cup vegetable oil
> 1/2 cup honey
> 1 cup milk
> 1/4 cup warm water

Turn liquid into dry ingredients and mix as for biscuits. Roll out to 1/4 inch thickness and cut desired size circle. Mark each bread with an X to facilitate breaking the bread. Bake for 15 minutes at 400 degrees F.

Art

1. As part of your study of the symbols found in the church building, have each student make a poster explaining some of the symbols.

2. The class might make a confirmation banner which could be carried or displayed at the service. Good resource books about banners are *Banners for Beginners* by Cory Atwood and *The Banner Book* by Betty Wolfe.

For Next Week: What materials do you need to provide for next week's lesson? Do the students need to bring anything?

There is one more theme remaining. What do you need to do to plan for a windup celebration? Adolescents love to eat! Do you want to plan for some special refreshments at the final session?

Remember to pray for your students during the coming week.

Theme Five
The Christian Life

Introduction

As Christians, we are asked to meet the demands of a Christian life-style. Our Christian faith changes the values we hold, the way we make decisions, the actions we choose or reject.

The Bible tells the story of God's relationship with human beings. In the Old Testament, we read God's laws for us as summarized in the Ten Commandments, and hear the call to right living in the words of the prophets. In the New Testament, we learn Jesus' teaching on how we should live, and read the letters written to early Christians to help them understand the demands of this way of life.

The Christian life has both a private and a public side. We are called to habits of daily life that include prayer, reading of the Scriptures, and participation in the worship of God. We also live in community, and so we are called to show our Christian faith. We are called "to strive for justice and peace among all people" (baptismal covenant). We are called to love and serve others, and to help build a just and caring society.

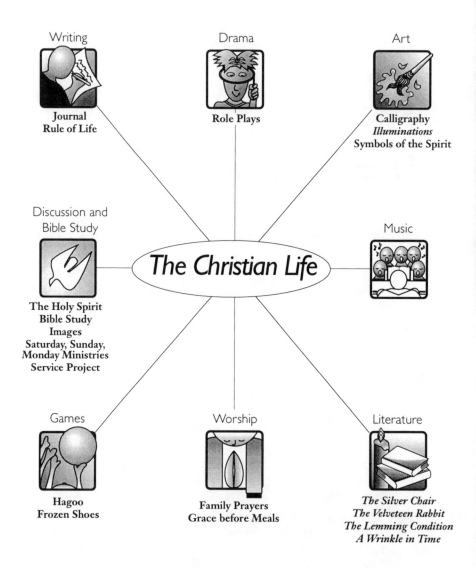

Writing
Journal
Rule of Life

Drama
Role Plays

Art
Calligraphy
Illuminations
Symbols of the Spirit

Discussion and
Bible Study
The Holy Spirit
Bible Study
Images
Saturday, Sunday,
Monday Ministries
Service Project

The Christian Life

Music

Games
Hagoo
Frozen Shoes

Worship
Family Prayers
Grace before Meals

Literature
The Silver Chair
The Velveteen Rabbit
The Lemming Condition
A Wrinkle in Time

Literature

The Velveteen Rabbit by Margery Williams. Read aloud to the class the following excerpt from *The Velveteen Rabbit*, in which the stuffed animals in a nursery talk about what it means to become real.

> The Skin Horse had lived longer in the nursery than any of the others. He was so old that his brown coat was bald in patches and showed the seams underneath.... "What is REAL?" asked the Rabbit one day, when they were lying side by side near the nursery fender, before Nana came to tidy the room. "Does it mean having things that buzz inside you and a stick-out handle?"
>
> "Real isn't how you are made," said the Skin Horse. "It's a thing that happens to you. When a child loves you for a long, long time, not just to play with, but REALLY loves you, then you become Real."
>
> "Does it hurt?" asked the Rabbit.
>
> "Sometimes," said the Skin Horse, for he was always truthful. "When you are Real you don't mind being hurt."
>
> "Does it happen all at once, like being wound up," he asked, "or bit by bit?"
>
> "It doesn't happen all at once," said the Skin Horse. "You become. It takes a long time. That's why it doesn't often happen to people who break easily, or have sharp edges, or who have to be carefully kept. Generally, by the time you are Real, most of your hair has been loved off, and your eyes drop out and you get loose in the joints and very shabby. But these things don't matter at all, because once you are Real you can't be ugly, except to people who don't understand."

"I suppose *you* are Real?" said the Rabbit. And then he wished he had not said it, for he thought the Skin Horse might be sensitive. But the Skin Horse only smiled.

"The Boy's Uncle made me Real," he said. "That was a great many years ago; but once you are Real you can't become unreal again. It lasts for always."

The Rabbit sighed. He thought it would be a long time before this magic called Real happened to him. He longed to become Real, to know what it felt like; and yet the idea of growing shabby and losing his eyes and whiskers was rather sad. He wished that he could become it without these uncomfortable things happening to him (pp. 12–16).

1. Ask your students:
   What does it mean to "become real"?
   Who do you know who is a real person?

2. Invite members of the class to complete the sentence, "A real person..." and record their ideas on a graffiti sheet; *or*

3. "Becoming real is like a worn much-loved toy." Ask the group what other metaphors they can think of. Have the students complete the phrase, "Becoming real is like..."

4. Becoming real sounds a bit painful. Ask the students:
   Where do you experience the hurts of becoming real?

The Lemming Condition by Alan Arkin. This is a short novel of only fifty-eight pages. If you can find a copy, you might want to read this aloud to your students. Here is a summary of the story:

Bubber wakes up early on the morning that the lemmings begin their great march West to jump in the ocean. He goes to say goodbye to Crow, and Crow begins to raise some questions about the trip. What happens after the jump? Can lemmings swim? Have any lemmings ever seen the ocean? Bubber tries to talk with the other lemmings, who caution him not to ask questions, just to go along with the crowd. He tries out the water in the pond and realizes that swimming is not for him. As the huge crowd of lemmings begins to move towards the cliff, Bubber at first feels the relief of being caught up in the crowd.

Read aloud the following excerpt:

> Fearful of what lay ahead, but even more afraid of complete isolation, Bubber threw himself into the crowd. It was defeat, and Bubber knew it, but it was mixed with great relief. All decisions were gone. So was concern for the future, so was the fear of conflicting with his own kind (ch. 6, p. 48).

Finally, he finds the strength to turn aside. "I'm not a lemming any more," he says. When asked what he is, he replies, "I'll let you know when I find out."

1. Ask the students the following questions:
   Why do you think that Bubber might get caught up in the lemmings' march to the sea?
   Why might he change his mind?
   Can you think of an occasion when you have felt pressured to go along with the crowd? What did you decide to do and why?
   Being a teenager is a time of finding out who you are. What are some of the things that help you to do that? Write in your journal what things you are finding out about yourself and what questions you have.

A Wrinkle in Time by Madeleine L'Engle. Outline the story for the students. Here is a sumary of the story:
   Meg Murry and her brother Charles Wallace need to go through a tesseract, a "wrinkle in time," to find their father and to rescue him from the evil powers which are

holding him captive. In a conversation with one of their helpers, Mrs. Whatsit, they talk about the meaning of free will within the pattern of our lives.

Read aloud the following excerpt:

Mrs. Whatsit sounded surprised at [Calvin's] question. "If we knew ahead of time what was going to happen we'd be—we'd be like the people on Camazotz, with no lives of our own, with everything all planned and done for us. How can I explain it to you? Oh, I know. In your language you have a form of poetry called the sonnet."

"Yes, yes," Calvin said impatiently. "What's that got to do with the Happy Medium?"

"Kindly pay me the courtesy of listening to me." Mrs. Whatsit's voice was stern, and for a moment Calvin stopped pawing the ground like a nervous colt. "It is a very strict form of poetry, is it not?"

"Yes."

"There are fourteen lines, I believe, all in iambic pentameter. That's a very strict rhythm or meter, yes?"

"Yes." Calvin nodded.

"And each line has to end with a rigid rhyme pattern. And if the poet does not do it exactly this way, it is not a sonnet, is it?"

"No."

"But within this strict form the poet has complete freedom to say whatever he wants, doesn't he?"

"Yes." Calvin nodded again.

"So," Mrs. Whatsit said.

"So what?"

"Oh, do not be stupid, boy!" Mrs. Whatsit scolded. "You know perfectly well what I am driving at!"

"You mean you're comparing our lives to a sonnet? A strict form, but freedom within it?"

"Yes." Mrs. Whatsit said. "You're given the form, but you have to write the sonnet yourself. What you say is completely up to you" (ch. 12, pp. 191–192).

1. Ask the students:
   What questions do you have about free will?
   Are there limits to our freedom?
   Are we free to do anything at all?
   Are our actions determined by something or someone else?

The Silver Chair by C. S. Lewis. Here is a summary of the story, followed by a passage to be read aloud to the class:
   Jill and Eustace are called by Aslan the lion into Narnia to rescue Prince Rilian from the evil witch. On this journey, they are accompanied by Puddleglum the marshwiggle. The witch tries to convince them that Narnia and Aslan do not exist. Here is Puddleglum's reply:

"One word, Ma'am," he said, coming back from the fire; limping, because of the pain. "One word. All you've been saying is quite right, I shouldn't wonder. I'm a chap who always liked to know the worst and then put the best face I can on it. So I won't deny any of what you said. But there's one thing more to be said, even so. Suppose we *have* only dreamed, or made up, all those things— trees and grass and sun and moon and stars and Aslan himself. Suppose we have. Then all I can say is that, in that case, the made-up things seem a good deal more important than the real ones. Suppose this black pit of a kingdom of yours is the only world. Well, it strikes me as a pretty poor one. And that's a funny thing, when you come to think of it. We're just babies making up a game, if you're right. But four babies playing a game can make a play-world which licks your real world hollow. That's why I'm going to stand by the play-world. I'm on Aslan's side even if there isn't any Aslan to lead it. I'm going to live as like a Narnian as I can even if there isn't any Narnia. So, thanking you kindly for our supper, if these two gentlemen and the young lady are ready, we're leaving your court at once and setting out in the dark to spend our lives looking for Overland. Not that our lives will be very long, I should think; but that's small loss if the world's as dull a place as you say" (ch. 12, pp. 156–157).

1. Puddleglum vows to live like a Narnian even though he is not certain that Narnia really exists. Ask the students:
   How can we live as Christians even if we have doubts and questions?

Saturday, Sunday, Monday Ministries

One way to look at our ministries is to see them in terms of some of the things we do each week. Our Saturday ministries are our leisure-time activities, sports, hobbies, family time. Our Sunday ministries might be a way of describing our church involvement—all those activities we do in the church building and as part of church programs. Our Monday ministries are those things we do at work or at school.

1. *Saturday*
   Ask the students:
   What does it mean to be a Christian in your leisure time? In sports or recreation? In community service? In family life?

2. *Sunday*
   Have the students brainstorm for a list of all the ways they and others are involved in the life of your parish. Ask:
   Which of these ministries are you doing?
   Are there any that you would like to do?
   What training and help would you need to take part in these ministries?

3. *Monday*

   Ask the group:

   What does it mean to be a Christian at school?

   Does it make a difference to the way you act?

   Would you feel comfortable saying grace in the lunchroom? In a restaurant?

   What are some of the ways in which young Christian people can make a difference?

   Is there a down side to this? What are some of the problems that being a Christian might cause you?

4. Have the students develop role plays about situations in which it is difficult to be a Christian.

Rule of Life

Here is one example of a rule of life: it is a pattern of Christian living set out in *The Book of Common Prayer* and *The Book of Alternative Services*. This example of a Rule of Life comes from the Diocese of Qu'Appelle. The portions in italics are drawn from the *BCP* (p. 555) and those in ordinary type are adapted from the baptismal covenant in the *BAS* (p. 159).

Thinking about a Rule of Life

Every Christian should from time to time frame a Rule of Life in accordance with the precepts of the gospel and the faith and order of the Church. In it, the following might be considered:

Regular attendance at public worship and especially at the Holy Eucharist; the practice of private prayer, Bible reading, and self-discipline.

   To continue in the apostles' teaching and fellowship, in the breaking of bread, and in the prayers.

Bringing the teaching and example of Christ into everyday life.

To seek and serve Christ in all persons, loving my
neighbour as myself; to persevere in resisting evil,
and, whenever I fall into sin, to repent and return
to the Lord.

The boldness of spoken witness to faith in Christ.

To proclaim by word and example the good news of God
in Christ.

Personal service to the Church and the community.

To strive for justice and peace among all people and to respect the
dignity of every human being.

*The offering of money according to means for the work of the Church in my
parish, the diocese, Canada, and overseas.*

1. Using this guideline, talk with the students about what might comprise their own personal rule of life.

2. Ask the students to draw up their own rule of life and write it in
   their journal. Have them pick one area to concentrate on in the
   coming week, and record their experience in their journal.

3. One of the habits of life is saying grace before meals. Here is a
   table grace which appears on materials from the Primate's World
   Relief and Development Fund:

   For food in a world where many are hungry,
   For friends in a world where many are alone,
   For faith in a world where many are afraid,
   We give you thanks, O God.
   Amen.

Ask the students:

Do you have a special grace before meals that your family uses?

Share other table graces. You will find graces in the BAS, pages 694 and 695.

4. Ask the students:

Does your family have any custom of saying family prayers together?

Both the BCP and the BAS have suggestions for family or home prayers. Your parish may be using *The Whole People of God* curriculum, which contains many suggestions for family activities and prayers.

Service Project

1. Select a project and involve the students in the experience of community service. Here are some suggestions:
   * help to prepare and serve a meal at the local soup kitchen
   * help out at the Food Bank
   * visit in a seniors' home or hospital
   * assist adult volunteers with the delivery of Meals on Wheels
   * help with a children's group.

2. When you return to the class, reflect with the students on the experience.

Mission Statements

The Anglican Consultative Council is a council of representatives from each of the thirty-seven member churches of the worldwide Anglican Communion. It has listed these areas of mission as important for Anglicans:

- the proclamation of the good news of the Kingdom;
- the teaching, baptizing, and nurturing of new believers;
- responding to human needs with loving service;
- transforming unjust structures of society;
- caring for and being a good steward of God's creation.

1. Discuss the following questions with the students:
   What can young people do in each of these areas?
   Does your parish or diocese have a mission statement?
   What might it mean to someone of your age?

Art

Have the students write their Rule of Life in calligraphy and illustrate it with border, perhaps illuminating the first letter as in a mediaeval manuscript. The picture book *Illuminations* by Jonathan Hunt is a good resource, or you may have pictures showing pages from the *Book of Kells* or other early manuscripts.

Drama

Have the students develop skits which show some of the difficulties and the strengths of being a Christian at school, in the family, in leisure time.

The Work of the Spirit

1. Wind and fire are images used to describe the Holy Spirit. Look at the Pentecost story in Acts 2:1–4. Ask the students:
   Why are these images appropriate to represent God the Spirit?

   Have them draw a picture with pastels which represents the symbols of the Spirit.

2. The description of Progo the cherubim in the novel *Wind in the Door* is of a creature composed of hundreds of wings and eyes and spurts of flame (ch. 3). Read this passage aloud to your students as they work.

Co-operative Games

Hagoo

Divide the students into two teams, which then stand facing each other. Two players, one from each team, face each other down the length of the lines. Each bows and solemnly says "Hagoo" to the other. They walk towards each other and past, to the opposite end of the line, looking their challenger in the eye and keeping an absolutely straight face. The teams try their best to get the other team's contestant to laugh. A challenger who completes the walk without smiling or laughing rejoins the team; if they laugh, they must join the other team. The game runs until all have had a turn. (Adapted from *The New Games Book* by Andrew Fluegelman, published by Doubleday Books.)

Frozen Shoes

Each person moves around the room while balancing an upside down shoe on his or her head. If the shoe falls off, the person is frozen until a friend comes to the rescue, picks up the shoe, and restores it—all the while keeping their own shoe balanced. For a more challenging game, play it in pairs or in small groups.

Discussion

1. Discuss the following questions with your students:

   Where do you see the Christian life as lived by others? This might be a bus driver, a coach, a clerk in a store.

   Where do you see evidence of the Christian life in public figures? In sports or pop figures?

2. Ask the students to keep an eye on the newspaper or magazines for examples from everyday life.

For next week: What do you and your students need to bring for next week? What have you learned from this session to help you with your planning for next week?

Remember your students and their families in your prayers during the coming week.

Final Event

If this is the final session, plan a special celebration to mark the end of your time together. You might want to bring in pizza or a special cake. Make a display of the students' work in the church or the hall. Is there some way in which students might share what they have learned in the worship service or with the rest of the parish?

Confirmation

If this material has been used to prepare students for confirmation, walk through the confirmation service with them so that they understand what the service will be like.

Try to incorporate into the service as much of the students' experience as you can—perhaps songs, art work, drama, movement.

Sometimes the bishop is able to be present at the confirmation rehearsal. This is a good opportunity for students to get to know the bishop and to ask any questions they may have.

Congratulate yourself on a job well done! You and your students have been together on a journey of discovery. Celebrate that, and give thanks for this class and for this opportunity to explore the faith together.

Appendix
What Does It Mean To Be an Anglican?

Who Are Anglicans?

Anglicans are people who belong to one of the branches of the world-wide Anglican Church. In Canada, Anglicans are members of the Anglican Church of Canada, a denomination of about a million members.

Anglican churches share a tradition of doctrine and worship as set out in *The Book of Common Prayer* and authorized alternative service books. In the Anglican Church there are a variety of traditions and practices—protestant and catholic, liberal and conservative. But we share many important things:

- a common order of ordained ministry—bishops, priests, and deacons;
- a common way of worshipping—regular Eucharists; the use of books of common prayer and of a lectionary; the sacraments of baptism, episcopal confirmation, the Eucharist, and other rites;
- a common heritage and tradition;
- the three cornerstones of Scripture, tradition, and reason.

The Anglican Communion

The Anglican Church of Canada is a member of the Anglican Communion. This is a group of thirty-seven member churches (called "provinces") which derived originally from the Church of England and which are connected by history, tradition, and custom. Representatives of the thirty-seven provinces meet together from time to time to share ideas and concerns. But each of the provinces makes its own independent decisions to order its life. The Anglican Church of Canada is a province, the Episcopal Church in the United States is another, the Church of England, the Church of the Province of Kenya, the Episcopal Church of Brazil are others. There are about seventy-five million Anglicans worldwide. Two books which describe the provinces are *Who Are the Anglicans?* (Forward Movement Publications) and *The Anglican Communion: A Guide* (Church House Publishing).

Each province is autonomous and governs its own life by its synods (parliaments of elected representatives). No decision by one province has authority over another province. However, the Archbishop of Canterbury holds a place of respect in the communion, as he represents the See or Diocese of Canterbury where St Augustine brought the Roman form of Christianity to England.

The Lambeth Conference is a gathering in which every diocesan bishop from around the world meets to discuss issues of concern. The conference is held every ten years and presently includes about eight hundred bishops. It has no legislative power but its statements carry a great deal of weight. Every diocese in the world has an equal share in these discussions.

The **Primates** (or chief bishops) of the thirty-seven provinces meet from time to time.

The Anglican Consultative Council is a gathering of bishops, priests, and lay people representing the thirty-seven provinces of the communion. They meet every three years to reflect on mission, ecumenism, doctrine, and social justice issues. It is the only international body where priests and lay people take part in discussions alongside the bishops. The Anglican Church of Canada has three members: a bishop, a priest, and a lay person.

All these gatherings are important ways of strengthening the life of the Anglican family. We have much in common with our Anglican sisters and brothers, and we need to foster these opportunities to learn from one another.

The symbol of the Anglican Communion is the compasrose with the Greek inscription, "The truth shall make you free."

What Do We Believe?

There are three standards of Anglican belief.

The Scriptures of the Old and New Testaments contain the essentials of our beliefs. They tell the story of how God acts in history and of how God's will is revealed to us in the life, death, and resurrection of Jesus Christ. The Prayer Book reminds us that "nothing may be taught in the Church as necessary to salvation unless it be concluded or proved [from Scripture]." Anglicans also read the deutero-canonical books (the Apocrypha) for edification. Anglicans have used the tools of biblical scholarship to help in studying and teaching the Scriptures.

Tradition helps us to understand Scripture. The Bible has been handed down to us by the community of faith. The historic **creeds** are traditional summaries of the Christian faith. The Apostles' Creed is the baptismal statement of faith and dates from about 200 A.D. The Nicene Creed arose from the church's attempt to deal with differences of belief and was formulated in the fourth century A.D. The Athanasian Creed is a long statement about the Trinity probably dating from the fifth century. It is seldom used in worship but is found in *The Book of Common Prayer.* The liturgy preserves a record of our tradition and belief. We proclaim what we believe in our prayers. Other parts of our tradition include theological writings.

Reason: Anglicans believe that God gave us the gift of reason and expects us to use our minds in studying and interpreting the scriptures and tradition. We need to apply reason also to the making of responsible ethical decisions. Anglicans place a good deal of value on informed common sense!

The Books We Use

Anglicans are a people of books. We follow an ordered form of worship as contained in *The Book of Common Prayer* or in other authorized texts such as *The Book of Alternative Services.*

The Book of Common Prayer

This is "common" prayer. We are a community of Christians who come together to worship using an agreed-upon form of words. Worship is not based on the whim of the ordained minister.

It is group prayer. There are few prayers purely for personal use. So prayers use "we" and "us" rather than "I" and "me."

The Prayer Book is based on the first books put together by Thomas Cranmer, Archbishop of Canterbury, during the sixteenth century. The book is revised from time to time. The most recent Canadian revision was in 1959. All provinces of the Communion have a Prayer Book, although they vary slightly from country to country.

The Prayer Book includes the Daily Office (Morning and Evening Prayer), the Eucharist (with accompanying Collects, Epistles, and Gospels), Baptism, the pastoral offices (Marriage, Burial of the Dead), the services conducted by a bishop (Confirmation, Ordination), the Psalter, and the Catechism. It offers a rich variety of prayers and readings, and contains within the words of the liturgy what Anglicans believe.

The Book of Alternative Services

Published in 1985, this is not a new prayer book but a collection of alternatives in contemporary English. The Baptism and Confirmation services reflect our growing understanding of the meaning of Christian Initiation. The Eucharist reflects the development of contemporary texts not just in our own church but in Anglican churches all over the world. The book does not contain everything that the Prayer Book did, as it is not intended as a replacement for the Prayer Book. So, for example, the Ten Commandments and the Catechism are not found in the newer book, but it is intended that parishes look for them in *The Book of Common Prayer*.

The Book of Occasional Celebrations 1992 contains models to be used in planning occasional services—blessing of a home, Advent, Christmas, and Easter festivals of lessons and carols, celebration of a new ministry, and so on.

Ministry

All are ministers. All baptized persons are part of the *laos*, the people of God, and are called to bring to others the good news of God's love. Lay men and women are active in many different kinds of ministry. Some people are called to special ministries in the church and are ordained with the laying on of hands and with prayers for the gifts of the Spirit to carry out that ministry.

The deacon is ordained to a ministry of service to others. Some people remain deacons on a permanent basis. Others are deacons for a period of time and then are ordained to the priesthood. Some deacons are in secular employment. But all the ordained have this ministry of service as the basis of their calling. Deacons have the title "Reverend" and may wear a clerical collar. They are not permitted to celebrate the Eucharist or to pronounce the absolution, but may read the gospel, preach, and baptize when licensed to do so. Deacons wear their stole across the left shoulder.

The priest or presbyter is ordained following a period as a deacon and is authorized to baptize, to celebrate the Eucharist, to hear confessions, and to pronounce the absolution. Priests may be placed in charge of parishes or may serve as chaplains or in other forms of ministry. Priests have the responsibility of care for all those within their jurisdiction. A priest is a member of a diocese, under the authority of the diocesan bishop, and shares with others responsibility for the life of the diocese. Priests wear their stole over both shoulders.

The bishop has oversight over the church in a particular diocese. There are thirty dioceses in the Anglican Church of Canada. Some have assistant bishops as well. Bishops are elected to their office by representative clergy and laity. Bishops represent the linking of the local church both historically, with the apostles and others commissioned by the early church, and in the present day, with all other Anglican bishops around the world. Bishops are pastors to the clergy and the laity. They ordain priests and deacons and assist in the ordination of other bishops. They appoint clergy to parish responsibilities. In the churches of their diocese they celebrate the rites of Christian Initiation, especially those affirming the baptismal covenant (confirmation, reception, the reaffirmation of baptismal vows). They chair meetings of synod and are responsible for the work of the church in that geographical area.

In the Anglican Church of Canada, all orders of ministry are open to both men and women. In the Anglican Church, there are **religious orders** of women and men who are bound by traditional vows of poverty, chastity, and obedience. They generally live in community and follow a regular rule of prayer. Their work may include conducting retreats and offering hospitality to guests, education, hospital work, and community service. The Church Army is a society of lay workers trained for ministries of evangelism and social service.

What People Wear

Clergy, and sometimes lay assistants, such as choir and servers, wear special robes for worship. These robes derive from the ordinary street dress of a gentleman of the early centuries. Christians fearing persecution tried to dress just like other people. But by the fourth century, certain garments came to be worn for religious rites and many of them we have retained in the present with very little change. The eucharistic vestments are the most ancient.

Alb—from "albus" (white). A long white robe, belted with a girdle or cincture (usually a rope or cord). At one time, the alb was worn only under the chasuble. Now it is common for Anglican clergy to wear only a cassock-alb with the stole.

Chasuble—is the principal eucharistic vestment. It is a poncho-like garment in the liturgical colour of the season.

Stole—a narrow strip of material in the colour of the season. It probably represents the towel with which Jesus girded himself as he washed the disciples' feet. Priests wear the stole around the neck and hanging down on both sides. Deacons wear the stole over the left shoulder.

The cassock and surplice are "choir dress," worn for the choir offices of Morning and Evening Prayer.

Cassock—A long robe, usually black but white in tropical countries. At one time, clergy wore the cassock as street dress. Choristers and servers also wear cassocks of any colour. Bishops wear purple cassocks.

Surplice—a shorter white robe worn over the cassock. Generally it has wide sleeves. The name came from the term "super pellicem," or something worn over the fur-lined cassock. It is also worn by choir members and servers.

Scarf—A strip of black material worn over the shoulders for the choir offices. It is sometimes called a "preaching scarf" or a "tippet." It probably derives from the academic hood. Clergy sometimes wear their academic hoods for Morning and Evening Prayer.

Bishops have distinctive vestments. The traditional colour associated with Anglican bishops is purple; so bishops generally wear purple shirts. A bishop wears an episcopal **ring** as a sign of the marriage of the bishop to the diocese. Sometimes the ring has a purple stone, an amethyst. The Greek word for amethyst means "not drunk" and refers to the description of the apostles at Pentecost (Acts 2:15). The ring may include the crest of the diocese, which may be used to imprint the bishop's seal on letters and official documents. Bishops also wear a **pectoral cross** (pectoral meaning worn on the chest). A bishop carries a **crozier** or pastoral staff, usually in the form of a shepherd's crook, as a sign of authority and jurisdiction in the diocese.

Cope—a long cape fastened with a clasp at the front, usually of precious material and elaborately decorated. Other clergy may also wear the cope in processions.

Mitre—a tall, divided hat worn by bishops. It is generally of precious material to match the cope. Its present shape symbolizes the tongues of flame which descended on the apostles at Pentecost. The two tabs of cloth which fall from the back of the mitre are called "lappets."

Bishops also have robes for non-eucharistic worship:
Rochet—a long white surplice worn over the purple cassock. It has full sleeves and may have ruffles at the wrist. These are the remains of the Elizabethan frill worn by all clergy.

Chimere—a sleeveless gown, generally scarlet, but it may also be black. It is similar to the doctoral gown.

What Clergy Are Called

Clergy use the title "The Reverend" as a sign of office. Strictly speaking, the title is an adjective and not a direct title of address. So it is correct to say "The Reverend *Mr.* Smith" or "The Reverend *Dorothy* Smith," but not "Reverend Smith." It is a good idea to ask clergy what they prefer to be called. Bishops may be addressed most simply as "Bishop Smith." There are old historical titles sometimes used—bishops as "My Lord" and archbishops as "Your Grace"—but these are now used less frequently.

Archbishop—("The Most Reverend") is the chief bishop of an ecclesiastical province. In Canada, there are four internal provinces—Canada, Ontario, Rupert's Land, and British Columbia. Each has an Archbishop with responsibilities for the oversight of the province and provincial synod.

The Primate—is the chief bishop of the Anglican Church of Canada. He is an archbishop but without territory. His office is at Church House in Toronto. He chairs General Synod, visits all parts of our church, and represents our church at national, international and ecumenical events.

The Bishop—("The Right Reverend") has the responsibility of the oversight of the church in a particular area called a **diocese**. A diocese may also have a co-adjutor bishop (one who will succeed the retiring diocesan bishop) or a suffragan, assistant, or area bishop (one who does not automatically succeed).

The Dean—("The Very Reverend") is generally rector of the cathedral. The cathedral has a special role in the diocese. It is the location of the bishop's "cathedra" or chair, a symbol of the bishop's role as chief pastor of the diocese. The cathedral is frequently the setting for special diocesan services and gatherings and is, in some sense, the "mother church" of the diocese. The dean has a role in the diocese as a senior priest, and frequently serves as the bishop's deputy in administrative matters if the bishop is out of the diocese.

Archdeacon—("The Venerable") is a priest with certain administrative responsibilities. The archdeacons assist the bishop in the day-to-day running of the diocese. Some archdeacons are parish priests and have responsibilities for geographical areas of the diocese. Some archdeacons work in the synod office as administrators.

Rural/Regional Deans—are clergy with some responsibilities for oversight within their deanery, a smaller area of the diocese. Regional deans call area clergy together for meetings. Sometimes the archdeacons and regional deans meet to advise and assist the bishop.

Canon—is an honorary title given to a priest or lay person in recognition of their dedicated service to the church. Canons have special seats in the cathedral and, in some cases, the canons along with the Dean form a "chapter" of clergy which governs the life of the cathedral.

What Is the Church?

The church is a community of men, women, and children, baptized into the Body of Christ, following Jesus in their daily life, committed to meeting together to worship God and to learn about God's will. Our participation in the life of the Christian community strengthens and enables us in the life of faith.

The term **church** is also used to describe a building. We generally meet in buildings consecrated by the bishop and set aside particularly for worship. Some Anglicans, however, meet in schools, in halls, and even in homes. The architecture and furnishing of churches may vary. Here are some of the traditional elements.

Parts of the building

The sanctuary ("holy place") is that part of the building, where the altar is located. It is often separated from the rest of the church by the altar rail.

The chancel ("singing place") is where the choir is traditionally located, although churches differ in this.

The nave ("ship") is the main body of the church where the pews or chairs are located. The ship of the church shelters and carries its members on their pilgrimage.

In a church which is shaped like a cross, the two side sections are called **transepts**.

Furniture

The altar ("altare"—up high) is the table where the Eucharist is celebrated. In Anglican churches, the altar is placed in a central position where it is the focus. In the Prayer Book, it is also called the Holy Table.

The font ("fountain") is where baptisms take place. It is often placed near the door of the church as a sign that it is by baptism that we become members of the Body of Christ and enter the Christian life. Sometimes a portable font is used at the front of the church so that everyone can see the baptism more easily.

The pulpit is where the sermon is preached. It is generally elevated so that everyone can see and hear.

The lectern is a stand which holds the Bible, from which the lessons of the day are read. Sometimes it is in the shape of an eagle.

Eucharistic vessels

The chalice is the large cup in which the wine is consecrated. It may be metal (silver or gold) or pottery.

The paten is the plate on which rests the bread to be consecrated.

Unleavened bread is generally in the form of wafers. Sometimes leavened bread is used. It may be broken from a loaf.

On the altar, the chalice and paten are covered by a **burse** and **veil** in the colour of the season. The burse holds the altar linen—the **corporal** (large white linen cloth) on which the chalice rests during the consecration and the **purificators** (small linen cloths) which are used by the administrators to clean the chalice. In most parishes, the altar guild sets up the communion vessels and cleans them after the service.

The bread and wine may be brought from the back of the church at the Offertory or may be brought to the priest by a server from the **credence table**, a small table beside the altar. On that table is also a container of water to mix with the wine, and sometimes water and a small bowl for washing the priest's hands before the consecration (the lavabo).

What Is a Sacrament?

A sacrament is described in the Catechism as "an outward and visible sign of an inward and spiritual grace" (*BCP*, page 550). God uses ordinary objects and actions to convey grace to us. Jesus used water, bread and wine, and the laying on of hands in sacramental ways, and the church continues to use these expressions of God's love and acceptance in obedience to God's will.

The two principal sacraments, Baptism and the Eucharist, are those which were commanded by Jesus during his ministry on earth.

Baptism is done with the pouring or sprinkling of water and in the name of the Trinity. In the Anglican Church, baptism may also be by immersion. Baptism signifies cleansing, the washing away of sin, and marks our incorporation into the death and resurrection of Jesus. It is the way in which we become part of the Christian community. Our Christian name is given to us in baptism. Through it we become "members of Christ, children of God and inheritors of the kingdom of heaven." Baptism may only be administered once to each person. Baptism requires us to make promises to turn from evil and to obey

God's will. Godparents or sponsors make these promises on behalf of infants. They have a responsibility to see that the child is brought up in the Christian faith, and represent the Christian community which is welcoming this new member. In the Anglican Church of Canada, it is recommended that baptism take place at the main service on a Sunday. Certain days are appropriate for baptism—Easter, Pentecost, All Saints Day, the Baptism of the Lord, and on the occasion of the bishop's visit.

In **the Eucharist**, the word is proclaimed and the bread and wine are consecrated to be shared by the people. In the consecrated bread and wine we believe that God's life is given to us. God becomes present to us in a special way through this sacrament. The Eucharist is a service of both Word and Sacrament. The Word is read and then broken open for the people by the preacher. The Sacrament is blessed by the prayers of the church and then broken by the priest for distribution to the people. The Eucharist follows a pattern of readings, prayers, thanksgiving, the repetition of the "words of institution" reminding us of Jesus' words and actions at the Last Supper, and the sharing of the bread and wine by all. The Eucharist has many names which emphasize particular aspects of its meaning. "Eucharist" means thanksgiving; we give thanks together for God's goodness and for God's grace given to us through the death and resurrection of Jesus. "Holy Communion" reminds us that we are in communion with God and also with one another. The Eucharist cannot be celebrated by one person alone; it always takes place in community. "The Lord's Supper" reminds us that it was Jesus who instituted this celebration and commands us to continue it. God calls us to the table. "The Mass" comes from the ancient words of dismissal "You have been sent"—and reminds us that the Eucharist strengthen us for Christian service in the world. Anglicans are required to be frequent in their participation in the Eucharist and are expected to receive communion every Easter at the very least. At one time, confirmation by a bishop was required before a person could receive communion. With a renewed understanding of baptism as admitting us to full membership in the church, baptized children and adults may now receive communion prior to confirmation.

At the end of the service, what remains of the bread and wine is reverently consumed. Some churches may keep consecrated bread and wine in a special place called an aumbry, to be used later for the communion of the sick. This is called the "reserved sacrament."

The Lesser Sacraments

There are five other rites, commonly called "sacraments."

Confirmation is the laying of on hands by the bishop with prayers for the gifts of the Holy Spirit for mission and ministry. It is a time when baptized persons take on the adult responsibilities for the Christian life and makes the baptismal promises for themselves. The presence of the bishop as minister of the sacrament connects each Anglican with the wider church. At one time, confirmation took place at twelve or thirteen years of age. Now that children may be admitted to Holy Communion at an earlier age, confirmation often takes place in late adolescence or in adulthood. The church is presently re-examining its practice of confirmation.

Reconciliation—we confess our sins regularly in our Sunday worship and receive absolution. Sometimes, however, we may wish to make to a priest an individual confession of sin and promise of amendment of life, and receive the assurance of God's forgiveness through the absolution. No one must make such a confession, but the sacrament is available to those who wish.

Marriage is the sacrament in which a man and a woman are joined together in physical and spiritual union. It includes the making of solemn vows, the giving and receiving of a ring, and the prayers for God's blessing on the marriage.

Ordination is the sacrament which sets a woman or man apart for particular offices and ministries in the church—the offices of deacon, priest, or bishop. The bishop lays hands on the candidates with prayers for the gifts of God's Spirit for the work to which they are called.

Anointing is a ministry of healing. It involves the laying on of hands with prayer and anointing with oil.

How We Are Governed

The parish is a geographical area in which a group of Anglicans meet together regularly for worship and community. A parish may consist of one congregation or many congregations. A priest is appointed by the bishop as rector/incumbent and has the responsibility for the life of the Christian church in that area. Lay people share many responsibilities in a parish—they help with worship, participate in education, care for the needs of parishioners, and maintain the church building. A parish council/vestry (lay people and clergy) meets regularly to make decisions about the life of the parish. The parish annual meeting of all parishioners allows everyone a share in decision-making.

The diocese is a geographical area under the leadership of the diocesan bishop. Every parish sends representatives to the diocesan synod which meets to discuss matters of concern to the church in the area. It elects a diocesan council/executive, which is able to make decisions between synods. Parishes contribute financially to the diocese for diocesan and national programs. Dioceses employ staff who work from the synod office to develop programs and administer the diocese. There are thirty dioceses in Canada.

The province is a larger area or region of Canada under the leadership of an archbishop. Dioceses send representatives to provincial synod to discuss issues of common concern. There are four provinces in Canada. The term is sometimes confusing because we also refer to the whole Anglican Church of Canada as a "province" of the Anglican Communion.

The national church is under the leadership of the primate. Dioceses send bishops, priests and lay people as representatives to General Synod which meets every three years to make decisions about the life of the Anglican Church of Canada. In between synods, decisions are made by the Council of General Synod. The work of the church is carried on through national staff at Church House in Toronto and through national committees of bishops, priests and lay people. The House of Bishops meets each year to discuss issues. The work of the national church is financed through the contributions of the dioceses.

(Previously published in *The Whole People of God* curriculum. Used by permission of Wood Lake Books, Inc.)

Resources

Books

Picture Books

Baylor, Byrd. *When Clay Sings*. New York: Scribners, 1972.

_____. *Everybody Needs a Rock*. New York: Atheneum, 1974.

_____. *The Way to Start a Day*. New York: Alladin, 1978.

Brooks, Diane. *Passing the Peace*. Ottawa: Penumbra Press, 1990.

Carrier, Roch. *The Hockey Sweater*. Montreal: Tundra, 1984.

Caton, Jacolyn. *The Potter*. Regina: Coteau, 1992.

Chase, Edith Newlin, and Ron Broda. *Waters*. Richmond Hill: Northwinds Press, 1993.

Frazier, Debra. *On the Day You Were Born*. New York: Harcourt Brace Jovanovich, 1991.

Getty-Sullivan, Mary Ann. *God Speaks to Us in Water Stories*. Collegeville: The Liturgical Press, 1996.

Hunt, Jonathan. *Illuminations*. New York: Bradbury Press, 1989.

Munsch, Robert. *Giant or Waiting for the Thursday Boat*. Willowdale: Annick, 1989.

Fiction

Arkin, Alan. *The Lemming Condition*. New York: Bantam, 1976.

Holm, Anne. *I Am David*. Harmondsworth: Puffin, 1969.

L'Engle, Madeleine. *A Wrinkle in Time*. New York: Dell, 1962.

_____. *A Wind in the Door*. New York: Dell 1973.

Lewis, C. S. *The Lion, the Witch and the Wardrobe*. Harmondsworth: Puffin, 1959.

_____. *The Magician's Nephew*. Harmondsworth: Puffin, 1963.

_____. *The Silver Chair*. Harmondsworth: Puffin, 1965.

Robinson, Barbara. *The Best Christmas Pageant Ever*. New York: Avon, 1972.

Williams, Margery. *The Velveteen Rabbit*. New York: Avon, 1975.

Non-Fiction

Atwood, Cory. *Banners for Beginners*. Harrisburg: Morehouse, 1986.

Best Recipes This Side of Heaven. Holy Trinity Church, Yorkton, Sask.

Bozarth-Campbell, Allah. *Womanpriest: A Personal Odyssey*. New York: Paulist Press, 1978.

Bradner, John. *Symbols of Church Seasons and Days*. Harrisburg: Morehouse, 1974.

Buechner, Frederick. *The Faces of Jesus*. New York: Harper & Row, 1974.

Emberley, Ed. *Ed Emberley's Great Thumbprint Drawing Book*. Boston: Little Brown, 1977.

Fluegelman, Andrew. *The New Games Book*. New York: Doubleday, 1976.

Haas, Ernst. *The Creation*. New York: Viking, 1971.

Kurelek, William. A *Northern Nativity*. Montreal: Tundra, 1976.

Lewis, C. S. *George Macdonald: An Anthology*. London: Geoffrey Bles, 1946.

_____. *Of Other Worlds*. New York: Harcourt Brace & World, 1966.

Macaulay, David. *Cathedral*. Boston: Houghton Mifflin, 1973.

Paterson, Katherine. *Gates of Excellence*. New York: Dutton, 1981.

_____. *The Spying Heart*. New York: Dutton, 1989.

Post, W. Ellwood. *Saints, Signs and Symbols*. Harrisburg: Morehouse, 1974.

Roberts, Elizabeth, and Elias Amidon. *Earth Prayers from around the World*. New York: Harper, 1991.

Songs for a Gospel People. Winfield, B.C.: Wood Lake Books, 1991.

Tindal, Mardi, and Kate Middleton. *Spirit of Singing*. Winfield, B.C.: Wood Lake Books, 1994.

The Book of Kells

The Hymn Book of the Anglican Church of Canada and the United Church of Canada. Toronto: Anglican Book Centre/United Church Publishing House, 1971.

The Whole People of God: Christian Education and Worship Resource. Winfield, B.C.: Wood Lake Books, published annually.

Wilson, Forrest. *What It Feels Like to Be a Building*. Washington: Preservation Press, 1988.

Winter, Miriam Therese. *WomanWitness*. New York: Crossroad, 1992.

_____. *WomanWisdom*. New York: Crossroad, 1993.

_____. *WomanWord*. New York: Crossroad, 1995.

Wolfe, Betty. *The Banner Book*. Harrisburg: Morehouse, 1874.

Books about the Anglican Church

Baycroft, John. *The Anglican Way*. Toronto: Anglican Book Centre, 1980.

Bays, Patricia. *This Anglican Church of Ours*. Winfield, B.C.: Wood Lake Books, 1995.

_____. *Meet the Family*. Toronto: Anglican Book Centre/Winfield, B.C.: Wood Lake Books, 1996.

Holmes, Urban T. *What Is Anglicanism?* Toronto: Anglican Book Centre, 1982.

Long, Charles Henry, ed. *Who Are the Anglicans?* Cincinnati, Ohio: Forward Movement Publications, 1988.

Stuchbery, Ian. *This Is Our Faith*. Toronto: Anglican Book Centre, 1990.

The Book of Alternative Services of the Angican Church of Canada. Toronto: Anglican Book Centre, 1985.

The Book of Common Prayer of the Anglican Church of Canada. Toronto: Anglican Book Centre, 1962.

The Anglican Church Directory. Toronto: Anglican Book Centre, published annually.

The Anglican Cycle of Prayer. Cincinnati, Ohio: Forward Movement Publications, published annually.

The Anglican Communion: A Guide. London: Church House Publishing, 1991.

Christian Initiation

A Gift for the Journey: A Baptismal Preparation Kit. Toronto: Anglican Book Centre, 1993.

Life in the Eucharist. Toronto: Anglican Book Centre, 1986.

Ross, Robert. *Preparing for Baptism*. Toronto: Anglican Book Centre, 1993.

Videos

Cottonpatch Gospel. Bridgestone Production Group, 1986.

Lewis, C.S. *The Lion, the Witch and the Wardrobe*. BBC, 1988.

Jesus Christ Superstar. MCA Home Video, 1986.

The Story of Anglicanism (three-video set). Cathedral Films and Videos.

Music

Debussy, Claude. "La Cathédrale Engloutie,": *Complete Piano Music Vol. 1*. Philips, 1993.

Holst, Gustav. *The Planets Suite*. EMI, 1974.

Hovhaness, Alan. *And God Created Great Whales*. Delos, 1970.

Pachelbel. "The Pachelbel Canon," *Albinoni Adagio*. RCA Victor, 1990.

Satie, Erik. *Oeuvres pour Piano—Pianoworks*. EMI, 1990.

Vangelis. *Chariots of Fire*. Polydor, 1981.